SEP 2 3 1990

D1068857

SOUL ON FIRE

ELDRIDGE CLEAVER

WORD BOOKS
PUBLISHER
WACO, TEXAS

EVANSTON PUBLIC LIBRARY
1703 ORRINGTON AVENUE
EVANSTON, ILLINOIS 60201

SOUL ON FIRE
Copyright © 1978 by Eldridge Cleaver.
All rights reserved. No portion of this book may
be reproduced in any form whatsoever without
written permission from the publisher, except
for brief quotations in reviews.

ISBN 0-8499-0046-8
Library of Congress catalog card number: 77-83335
Printed in the United States of America

This book is dedicated to the proposition that all human beings are created equal—in sin—with the God-given capacity to rise above themselves. From the depths of the pit of despair we can ascend to sublime heights of hope and fulfillment. Not to gild the lily but to point the Way, I dedicate this book to that loving proposition, Jesus Christ, our Lord and Savior, who can do for everyone what he did for me.

ACKNOWLEDGMENTS

I salute the long-suffering patience of the wonderful brothers and sisters at Word with whom I worked to bring this book from dream to reality. Jarrell McCracken, being the boss, didn't really need the patience of Job. That could have been left to my editor, Floyd Thatcher, who came through for me when I should have been coming through for him. Pat Wienandt is the unsung heroine of this tale. She put the nuts on the bolts.

But all this would have gone for naught but for the selfless assistance of David Poling, a vari-talented presbyterian minister from the lonely outpost of Albuquerque, New Mexico. Dave cross-examined me for thirteen hours, unearthing the raw material in the dusty bins of my mind. Thanks, Dave.

And thank you, Lord, for sending your saints my way.

CONTENTS

SOUL ON FIRE

1

SOUL ON FIRE

THE TWA 747 FLIGHT from Paris' Orly International Airport to New York's John F. Kennedy, seemed like the longest trip I had ever taken. Returning to America after seven years in exile filled me with trepidation. I was looking into the unknown, comforted by the knowledge that *it was all right*. Which doesn't mean that things were working out according to *my* plan. But rather that despite the fact I had no plan at all, still *it was all right!*

Instead of dreading the unknown, I've always looked upon it as a potential for increase, a source from which to draw knowledge and experience. But I was looking forward with the deepest dread to the unknown prison cell awaiting me. There was nothing I wanted in the potential

of a prison cell. The prospect of finding myself inside one
again, after having had so many years of freedom that I'd
gotten used to it, excited neither my curiosity nor my keen
enthusiasm for adventure. The only unanswered question,
which I dreaded even to pose to myself, was whether or
not I could still endure the toughest, practical aspects of
confinement: like, in the wee hours, could I, still, as I
had done through fourteen years in jails; reform schools;
adjustment, classification, and detention centers; and state
prisons—could I still, when the walls closed in, when I
yearned for a breath of fresh air, locked inside that can,
when the entire body and being cries out that the door
must be opened—could I still find the ability not only to
endure, but to prevail? The fourteen years already under
my belt were enough not only to burn me out on the sub-
ject of imprisonment, but to ignite in me a flaming love
of freedom and an unquenchable yearning for personal
liberation. *Now I was seated between two FBI agents, one
black and one white, who would formally arrest me when
we landed in New York, closing my wrists in circles called
handcuffs, cloaking my life in new mysteries.*

My deepest satisfaction was that I had not been captured, and therefore, was not returning yoked with the
humiliation of that defeat. My exaltation on this point
went beyond the exhilaration and repose found by those
who've lived just one step ahead of the law for so long
that they take the breath of the law on the nape of their
neck for the prevailing winds over their terrain. There is a
point of pride in any man who terminates seven years as
a fugitive with the voluntary act of surrender. From Cuba
to Algeria, from the imperial gates of People's China to
the tombstone balconies of Moscow, I had been in free-
flow control of my revolutionary destiny. I was pleased
with some of the choices I had made. I knew that the
world would look at me and be unable to distinguish be-

tween growth pains and death throes. I was in motion. A game fowl—a jailbird—in plumage black and red, had broken cover, had risen from its sanctuary in the land of the Gauls.

The public reaction was predictable: folks would close their eyes and plug up their ears with their fingers, so that later on they could truthfully say they had heard neither the rifles of the firing squads nor the screams of the dying. When they opened their eyes and unplugged their ears again, they would all give their versions of what happened. And I would give mine. Mine would be rejected, until all the blind and deaf ones fell.

I was buoyed up by a great secret light both within and outside me. In death throes was a vision of the cause; in growth pains was the cause itself—the true liberation of all humankind enslaved for whatever reason. Organizations are dedicated to visions of causes, to the implementation of particular visions, while one's self should be dedicated to the cause. But causes can grow either larger or smaller. A general law of causes may be that their toxic content gains potency in proportion to their shrinkage in volume. Outworn organizations are not half as malignant as worn-out causes.

I was no longer a member of any organization except my family, and the secret new world of light. I was free of the old Black Panther vision of our cause. The cause itself had grown beyond all my old vistas, and I was on the upward curve of a new arc. The cause had trembled in a spasm of new birth and dazzling new light. The myth of International Proletarian Solidarity, which seems must die each generation, was dead. Suicide or murder—it was gone. The Black Panther Party was dead, its image transmuted into capital in the political coffers of the Democratic Party. It was truly the end of an era.

During those last days in Paris and first days back in the

USA, my thought was in a holding pattern. Conclusions, premises for later actions, were being stored up in the nerves. The war in Vietnam, at last, was over! But now another struggle, in Vietnam, was joined! Conundrums. Humpty Dumpty sat on the wall. . . . *Only* the king's men can . . . put Richard Nixon back together again. . . . Perhaps those intellectual and moral tragedies should have enhanced my satisfaction as well. I had been given awareness and understanding of all the fraudulent promises. I had been spared the final wasting of my life on gods that not only had failed, but had pulled all the triggers on all the guns on all sides of all the arguments since the beginning of strife.

I liked the idea of rising to the occasion. I thought of myself as a gambler who has had a rough night. It was out of anguish and despair that I clung to that image. (Some hearings were under way in Washington, as the Church Committee inquired into the illegal activities of the FBI and CIA, which colored some of the jokes passed between myself and my FBI companions. "We may as well get along with each other," someone said. "We may wind up in the same cell together.")

I stood in awe of the compelling changes taking place within America itself. It was like watching Big Brother becoming Uncle Sam—the white face of death taking on a human hue; white-bearded wisdom, striped pants offering a feeling of hope and possibility.

What else? J. Edgar Hoover had gone on to his reward. I was strangely aware of the lack of enmity in my memory of him. I was suspicious of my lack of enmity towards anything. Suspicious over how happy I was to be going home. *Going home!* Powerful stuff, any time, any place, anywhere.

I had not planned it, but it was a boon to my search for a soft landing, that President Ford left Paris the same day

I did, at the end of a visit with French President Valéry Giscard d'Estaing. Ford took another plane than mine, but many of the journalists who'd been dogging his trail flew back with me in the anxious democracy inside the nose cone of the 747.

But most of all, folks in America had changed, and I felt that there were possibilities for me in the 1980s, and the 1970s were just half done. Everything was going to be all right!

THE WORLD OF the late 1960s raced through my mind as the 747 soared toward New York. The era of street gunfire and glass breaking and cities burning. Of bombings in Hanoi, in Hartford. Vivid still, that decade of death in Vietnam and the warfare that soaked our ghettos in America . . . the public murders of Martin Luther King, the Kennedy brothers, the gunning down of Malcolm X. All this crowded through my mind, had to be gathered up and put away . . . along with some words I said back in 1968: that if by some quirk of circumstance, I should be elected President on the Peace and Freedom Party ticket, I would not enter the White House, but would burn it down, erecting on its ruins a museum or monument to the decadence of the past. . . .

In those seven years a war finally was shut down in Asia and Richard Nixon barely missed his impeachment party. We Panthers had expected a military coup to take management of "American democracy," that being the only appropriate response of the people in charge to the revolutionary war exploding all over North America. I had also believed that a significant group of urban guerrillas would emerge from the returning veterans of Vietnam, most of them black, but many of them white or Chicano, traumatized and enraged by the imperial savagery of Washington's policy in Vietnam. They would soon be turning automatic weapons against what we had considered the real enemy, the pig power of America. Black Panther forces were increasing, weapons were being stored all over black communities, young people trained in the use of sophisticated armaments and a grand strategy unfolding that would plunge the United States into open civil war.

How different was my return from the one we had discussed in long planning sessions in Algeria! Then we had envisioned entering through the mountains of Mexico and forming guerrilla bases in the Rocky Mountain West, expanding eventually to other bases in the Alleghenies and Appalachians, to the Blue Ridge Mountains. The mountains were the people's fortress, and the American people had been blessed in that regard. The early vision was to create a training center in Cuba for insurgent forces and to mount a return from there. What Castro had done in the Sierra Maestra Mountains as a step in his overthrow of Batista, we felt we should try. We would trigger a general uprising and go on to save America from the fascist dictatorship looming on the horizon. Mao Tse-tung had fallen back upon the mountains after Chiang Kai-chek had slaughtered his forces in Shanghai. Kim Il Sung had led a fifteen-year guerrilla war against the Japanese from the sanctuary of the North Korean mountains. Tito of Yugoslavia had survived in the mountains of his country. A line from a song I wrote exhorted:

> Come out, come out, you bright-eyed warriors
> Face to face with our destiny
> Let's show the world how to fight for freedom
> In the cities and wilds of Babylon
> We'll take a long march to the top of the mountains
> And tear down this empire of Babylon. . . .

Those were out of my Little Red Book days. The Communist manuals had become our bible, our blueprints for survival and then success.

Yet, here I was, free of all chains, returning to a federal prison in California, to a trial that now was nearly a decade in waiting, reliving the dread of being slaughtered

in jail, perhaps, by some police revenge—or some old ac-
counting by the Communists, or a sick gangster, or a fiend
out for the rare bird of paradise, or his name in the news.
Yet somehow I was beyond all fear, beyond the restraints
of self-protection or the paranoia of earlier confinement,
for I was at last trusting in the Spirit of God to lead me.
I wasn't sure at that time how or where, but I had taken
the plunge. There was no turning back now.

WHILE MUCH OF THE commotion and violence of the sixties is known to most of you readers, what you may not know is the specific reason for my swift departure from California to New York, then Canada and underground in Cuba. The Black Panthers were in a stage of open hostilities with law enforcement agencies. J. Edgar Hoover himself had pronounced from on high that the Black Panther Party was the number one internal threat to the United States of America, a dubious status. Translated from FBIese, it meant that the Black Panthers were officially and publicly certified as fair game, and if anybody doubted, it now was clear that we were at the top of Hoover's hit list. Our homes were ransacked, our offices were under constant surveillance and often fired upon from speeding cars, our telephones were tapped and our every move tracked by the informers working for the Hoover-then Mitchell-Nixon confederation of repression.

On January 16, 1968, my apartment in San Francisco was searched top to bottom by the San Francisco Tactical Squad, who had entered in the first place by kicking down my front door in proper Gestapo fashion. Across America, black people were at the end of their patience with the empty promises and fulfilled threats of a government which now seemed prepared to wage war in the ghetto with the same mindlessness that it continued to kill Vietnamese. The summer before, riots broke out in the depressed neighborhoods of Newark, New Jersey, and twenty-six people were dead when the firestorm subsided. In Detroit, the same July month, five thousand people were homeless after the urban riots which claimed forty lives and brought in a division of the National Guard. White America was on edge, yes, but black America was being pushed over the edge.

The final shock did not come until the spring evening of April 4, 1968, when Martin Luther King was murdered by a high-powered rifle on a Memphis motel balcony. Who should be surprised that hard-pressed black people everywhere took to the streets in protesting rage? King was not just another nigger, and while in those days I had not believed that nonviolence could accomplish anything worth keeping, his peaceful protests had set the stage for a new era of black awareness and dignity.

In response to the outpouring of rage and destruction by the black community, LBJ called out the troops to get Washington back under control. And in 29 other states, at least 125 cities blew up with fresh expressions of black rage. The Panthers were right—we were in a state of siege. Hoover used the King assassination as a perfect setup to nail the black revolutionary groups that he could not constitutionally shut down or squeeze off. What better moment than this to pump up all the jittery local cops and state troopers, sending a special top-secret alert around the horn to have us in the gun sights of his fellow men in blue?

Two nights after Martin Luther King's murder, three carloads of Black Panthers were driving slowly through an Oakland neighborhood. Bobby Hutton and I were in the lead car. We were going to a friend's house. In this period, I never dared travel alone. We were certain that the Oakland and Alameda County Police had a death squad operating—sort of a select group dedicated to knocking off Panthers when time, place, and conditions allowed. With no witnesses. Or where it was the cops' word against "known criminals." And, by then, we were known and about to be blown.

We were walking on eggshells and knew it. We expected

to be killed at every moment. And although we were afraid, we were ready to lay down our lives that our people might live in peace and freedom. There was a chance encounter between a three-car convoy of Black Panther Party members and an Oakland Police Department cruiser. Red lights flashing in the night. Guns blazing in the dark. The whole world seemed to erupt in gunfire. Bobby and I ran to a vacant house, and the others who knew the neighborhood ran through the lot and over some fences. We were immediately pinned down with rifle fire and tear gas. In the first few minutes I was smacked in the chest and knocked unconscious by a tear gas shell. Hutton tore off my shirt to see if I was wounded or bleeding. I was only stunned and woke up to another hour and a half of gas, shooting, and sirens. Police came from surrounding areas—Emeryville, Contra Costa county. . . . I was shot in the leg, and we were both near suffocation from the gas, which finally exploded into a bellowing sheet of flames.

We were trapped. We yelled out that we were coming out to surrender. The whole residence was bathed in police spotlights. There were armed officers with semiautomatic weapons all around—and up on the roof of the building next door. My shirt was off, and my pants were rolled up where I was trying to stop the bleeding in my leg.

As I limped forward (reports of my being naked were exaggerated), one cop called me a name and told me to run to the paddy wagon. This was the Witches' Hour, the moment of truth. I was sure this man wanted to kill me, that he had already sentenced me to death in his heart. He wanted me to run to give him a pretext for shooting, the oldest and dirtiest cop trick of all, the use of which turns some guardians of the law into wanton murderers, enemies instead of friends. "Look, man," I said, "I'm wounded and bleeding. I can't run." He started kicking me on my wounded leg.

A policeman gave Bobby a shove toward the paddy wagon, and as he stumbled down a slight incline, about ten cops cut loose with their weapons. Little Bobby was dead before he reached the ground.

Then the police hustled me inside the dark cavity of the wagon and started beating me with their pistols. The anger, rage, frustration of the hour was getting to them—on me. Over the speaker, the police radio operator asked them what was happening, what was going on. One was dead, they said, and they had one under arrest. A voice asked over the radio who was handcuffed? So I said Eldridge Cleaver. I had learned from observing the evidence presented in Huey Newton's trial that all communication over the police radio is recorded on a continuous tape. The tape would show that I had been alive inside that van. They were ordered to stop working me over.

That one and a half hours on April 6, 1968, was to propel me into seven years of exile. I was convinced that a return to prison in Alameda County on a parole violation charge, which had been ruled invalid by California Superior Court Justice Raymond J. Sherwin, was tantamount to a sentence of death. So I fled, not just for my own skin, but out of an unwillingness to knuckle under, to be cut down through a possible perversion and distortion of our system of justice.

IN THE PASSING of the last ten years, I can see more clearly why my ideas were so inflammatory to so many people. Opposition to the war in Vietnam bitterly divided the country. It was an incendiary era. A bonfire ignited by generations of smoldering rage among the black, deprived people of North America. There were and are millions of other deprived, dispossessed, and put-down peoples in the world, many of whom I have seen and some of whom I have known. But the largest sorrow was my own ghetto family life, the people across the street and the kids down the avenue who were not going to have any chance to be anything in this police state which controlled our lives.

Anyone with real sensitivity in human relationships and even the slightest grasp of the daily depression of racial victimization must admit that the Black Panthers of the sixties became the hope and honor of millions of Negroes in America. Without the nerve-wracking resistance of the Black Panther Party, I believe there would have been a setback in the advance in meaningful civil rights.

So much misunderstanding and so many outright dishonest descriptions of the Black Panthers exist that some misconceptions must be set straight: we were essentially a political action party, dedicated to serving the people. Ever since the Watts uprising of 1965, in which scores of black people had been killed, a rising tide had been growing against what had every appearance of the indiscriminate killing of citizens by the police. Everyone *talked* about it but no one was *doing* anything about it. The Black Panther Party was called into being by this, strongly dedicated to organizing resistance to the repression from the occupying army of police that patrolled the black community like foreign troops. We believed that no political or social change could develop as long as the Gestapo power of the police could intimidate a speaker, writer, or organization.

As a result, we became the target, the lightning rod, for every shock wave that bounced back from a threatened white power structure. I knew, as did Seale and Newton, that it would require large doses of courage and a certain reckless attitude toward death to make a dent in the massive white/police manipulation of the black neighborhood. The very first thing that happened was the creation of armed black patrols that followed the cops around the ghetto and monitored *their* conduct. When a black man or woman was shoved up against a wall or spread across the hood of a car, our Panthers would jump out and focus immediate community attention on the encounter. We would advise the victim of his constitutional rights, with the cops snorting and swearing at us, threatening all sorts of bad things for being around. But it began to work. The police got furious, but we gained the respect and admiration of millions of blacks for having the guts to face up to these bullies and urge others to do the same.

The opposition and most of the people in charge tried to smear us and put the gangster label on our activities and behavior. Yet when the hottest, most desperate hours fell on the black community following the death of Martin Luther King, I went to a junior high school in Oakland and talked the kids, who were in a mindless fury, out of burning the place to the ground. I told them there were responsible ways that a caring, determined black youngster could more fully honor the ideals of that martyred preacher.

Our cry was (and still is) for dignity, freedom, and pursuit of happiness—something that black leaders have cried out for and pointed to for centuries. The only difference was that we had guns—that beautiful constitutional right to own arms—and we laid it squarely on the line for white America, especially white police-power America, because they knew better than anybody else what a gun could accomplish. And while they hated us for our unflinching bravado, they both respected and feared us.

In 1976, the U.S. Senate Select Committee on Intelligence Activities (the Church Committee) reported that the FBI had "initiated a covert program to disrupt and neutralize organizations which it characterized as black nationalist hate groups."

During the same period of investigation, the *New York Times* noted: "The Federal Bureau of Investigation carried out a secret, nationwide effort to destroy the Black Panthers, including attempts to stir up bloody gang warfare between the Panthers and other groups, and to create factional splits within the party."

They succeeded, and had hosts of helpers working with them in the lethal destruction of our constitutional rights as well as our lives. (This is why in 1976 we could file a 4.5 million dollar damage suit in Federal Court in San Francisco against Charles Bates, former special agent for the FBI, the estate of the late J. Edgar Hoover, as well as former Attorneys General John Mitchell and Richard Kleindienst, former CIA Director Richard Helms, and former Postmaster General Winton Blount. One result is that we have access to files of information vital to my defense.)

Once the liquidation lever had been pulled, the word sent out, it's only by Providence that I am alive to talk about it. You could hear the time bomb ticking, you could feel the closing in of police forces, you would soon see the result of their master plan. First it was the set up to put Huey Newton into a position where a shoot-out would occur—it did in October of 1967, and a cop was killed and Huey wounded and convicted and sentenced to from two to fifteen years. Then on January 15, 1968, David Hilliard, the Black Panther staff leader for office management, was arrested while handing out leaflets at a school in Oakland. The following day police kicked their way into my apartment and searched it without a warrant. In early February, a Panther and his date were arrested at a peace rally, for disturbing the peace, which, I gather, was caused by listening to Dr. Spock.

They were both beaten while in jail, and the pace quickened and sickened. In late February, same year, 1968, Jimmy Charley, another Panther, approached a cop who was working over a black person and was promptly arrested for, yes, "resisting arrest." The next day, February 25, police kicked in the front door of Bobby Seale's place; it was 3:30 A.M. and, of course, they had no search warrant. Do you see how we knew we were into warfare, that self-protection and arms became our only image to the outside world that had no grasp of what was going on inside our real world?

Of course, the little dramatization that the Panthers pulled off on the California Assembly in Sacramento, where twenty-four armed blacks walked into the presence of the lawmakers who were discussing the right to bear arms—it was mind-blowing and attention-getting. And the legislators were in a cold sweat. Just think of it, they said, those twenty-four black punks walking in here with shotguns and deer rifles—we could have been killed. Our point was that they were not killed, but in our wilder, most desperate moments, we had plenty of ideas about shooting up Congress, attacking the White House and taking over the government. The earlier Puerto Rican terrorist adventure during the Truman period gave us some clues. But our death wish was held in check and the California Assembly promptly passed new laws covering such lethal appearances—even added a whole new security force around the State House grounds. More than one officer has thanked me for creating his new job in Sacramento . . .

But no one seemed to care a flick about the life, limb, or security of black people, especially if you were a young, black, ghetto-bound person, and very especially, if you were a member of the Black Panthers.

We were no longer talking about police repression, or police brutality, or getting roughed up on Saturday night, or punched on the way to the lockup. We were experiencing murder—our members were walking through a shooting gallery all across America. It started that night when Bobby Hutton and I were shot up in Oakland:

Name	Age	Date of Death	Place
Bobby Hutton	17	April 1968	Oakland
*Tommy Lewis	18	August 1968	Los Angeles
*Robert Lawrence	22	August 1968	Los Angeles
*Steve Bartholomew	21	August 1968	Los Angeles
Frank Diggs	41	December 1968	Long Beach
Arthur Morris	28	January 1969	Los Angeles
John Huggins	23	January 1969	Los Angeles
Alprentice Carter	26	January 1969	Los Angeles
John Savage	21	May 1969	San Diego
Alex Rackley	24	May 1969	New Haven
Larry Roberson	21	July 1969	Chicago
Sylvester Bell	34	August 1969	San Diego
Nathaniel Clark	19	September 1969	Los Angeles
Walter Pope	20	October 1969	Los Angeles
Welton Armstead	17	October 1969	Seattle
Sidney Miller	21	November 1969	Seattle
Spurgeon Winters	19	November 1969	Chicago
Fred Hampton	21	December 1969	Chicago
Mark Clark	22	December 1969	Chicago

* All killed in Los Angeles, their deaths ruled "justifiable homicide."

It seemed amazing to us that the media identified the Black Panthers as cutthroats and outlaws, taunting the police and disturbing the peace: *we* were the ones who were going to funerals every month and living with the threat of immediate extermination by the police. Our very resistance and pugnacity seemed to drive them to further rage, especially when they started picking on returned Vietnam soldiers who were prepared for their moves and successful in withstanding their concerted attacks.

By now metropolitan police departments, with CIA and FBI coaching and stirring, were hitting our headquarters and residences with pre-dawn, come-in firing attacks. They long since had given up on the warrant-search routine. They cooked up alibis for blasting into our homes, apartments, offices; and when we would return the fire in self-defense, we were blamed for sniping at cops. It was in this scenario that a Vietnam veteran we called Geronimo proved most effective.

He had Panther families—and office personnel—bring empty gunnysacks into their homes. These were filled with dirt from the basement and then placed two feet thick all around the inside of the building, up to window level. Outside the office or residence looked plain jane; inside, it was a fortified bunker and could stop machine gun bullets. And well they did, for on December 8, 1969, four days after the police raid on the homes and offices of the Chicago branch of the Black Panther Party in which Fred Hampton and Mark Clark were brutally killed, the Los Angeles Police Department hit our headquarters with a sunrise attack, but were met with a withering hail of return gunfire. Geronimo's sandbags stopped everything that was thrown at us. Then came the tear gas, but Geronimo was way ahead of them. He had stored surplus gas masks and these were quickly put on, so the exchange of shooting kept up all day. Finally the television people arrived and the community people started yelling by the thousands, and the cops realized that these games were just not going to work.

Amazingly, no one was killed, and a cease-fire was established and a surrender worked out. It was obvious to everyone that the Panthers had simply been attacked; and when the case came up in court, it was thrown out. Geronimo fled to Texas, knowing that he was marked for being so clever with armaments and defense. He was finally captured and the police in California put all kinds of charges on him. Right now he is serving a sentence for a murder he didn't commit, and there is enough evidence from the Church Committee investigation to reopen his case and reveal the rigging, the paid informing, and the false witnesses responsible for his imprisonment. Many of the deaths of Panther people were outright executions, staged to appear justified—like the phony shootout of Bunchy Carter and John Huggins at UCLA. The Church Committee files have all the records—right down to the memos that were sent back to J. Edgar Hoover on the hard work that was done and how well it finally had paid off. Welcome to America.

It has been said that the military and naval leadership of the British Empire which fought with such determination in World War I and World War II was established on the playing fields of Eton and Harrow. My games were played in the ghetto of East Los Angeles, preceded by a few hazy memories of Little Rock, Arkansas, and a blazing year in Phoenix, Arizona, where I did my rite of passage.

2

CHILDHOOD
LESSONS

ARKANSAS WAS A perpendicular cliff of red clay in our backyard. Our house straddled the edge of this cliff, with the
back porch sticking out into empty space, resting on long
stilt supporting timbers, rising up from the black dirt of
our backyard below. I do not remember how high up the
porch was, except that it was equal to the height of the
cliff, all of it something happening over my head. I can peg
these moments in time with images of my baby brother,
Theophilus, five years my junior, wearing diapers and
sucking on his bottle, marking me as five or six years old.
Suddenly I was there, playing in the clay out of which
mother said we had been formed. I still recall the vital,
pungent odor of the soft clay, its cool texture. How good
it felt when squeezed through fingers and toes.

Big black bumblebees, with yellow stripes across their backs, made their homes in holes in the clay. As they emerged from their holes, we sometimes trapped them in glass jars, watched them searching in confusion for a way out, and listened to their distressed buzzing through air-holes punched in the tin lids. More than once I must have spied a lizard sneaking into the old water pipe sticking out of the clay at about the level of my eyes, and more than once I must have flushed him out with a long stick, or with a stiff stream of hot pee pee artfully directed, sending the lizard scurrying for higher ground.

When Theophilus, sitting on the back porch at the top of the stilts, fell off, landed in the clay, and never even stopped sucking his bottle, the value of the clay could only have been enhanced in my eyes. I remember neither when I started nor when I stopped eating the clay, only my mother's shrill voice prophesying doom if I didn't stop. I can still see the little dark hands, feet, and legs of brothers, sisters, and perhaps friends, as over the years we shaped the world with our hands.

Years later, long after we were gone from this house at the source, great tidal waves of red gooey muck rushed at me in a recurring bad dream. In the dream I was always fleeing, or flopping about, always on the verge of being overwhelmed.

We were five children then, two girls and three boys, offspring of Leroy Cleaver and Thelma Hattie Robinson united in Holy Matrimony in 1926. I list us in rank by birth:

Wilhelmina Marie	October 21, 1926
Helen Grace	May 3, 1932
Leroy Eldridge	August 31, 1935
James Weldon	October 10, 1937
Theophilus Henry	December 9, 1940

There was great antagonism between the Cleavers and the Robinsons—going back, to my knowledge, at least to my grandfathers on both sides. They had been called, they said, by God Almighty, to preach the true gospel to their people. The difference between these two gentlemen was the classic dichotomy between black people in America, with roots that go back into slavery. Grandpa Robinson was a House Nigger and Grandpa Cleaver was a Field Nigger.

Grandpa Robinson was part of a great tribe of mulattos. They were proud of their grey-blue eyes and pointed noses, and alluded to the white and Indian blood in their veins. They ran rumors around in circles of cousins who were passing for white, about one who had married and disappeared into the white race, leaving not a trace behind, except them. Grandpa Robinson was the pillar in the Little Rock branch of his tribe. St. Andrews AME was an important church in town. He was the first to make Little Rock work for the Robinsons, and his success enabled others of his tribe to pluck up their roots in Hot Springs and Pine Bluff and migrate to Little Rock.

Grandpa Cleaver was the very opposite of Grandpa Robinson. Tall and black-skinned, he had a house that sat in the middle of a cotton farm, and he did his shopping at the company store. He raised hogs, chickens, and vegetables, and is said to have sired several families besides the one from whence my father came. The old lady I knew as Grandma is said to have been about his third wife. He lived to be 98 years old. This old man, rooted in Malvern and Camden, had been a CC rider, a circuit-riding preacher who had traveled for years throughout the region, preaching the gospel as revealed to him. He had finally settled down in Wabbaseka, which must be one of the smallest dots on any map of Arkansas. As in our house my father's piano was untouchable, his father's holy of holies was an old typewiter, and if you touched it you would go directly to hell, with a broken tail.

Mother met Father because both of their fathers were working the soul circuit, and there were conventions, picnics, and various other get-togethers. Perhaps. But my father was capable of running my mother to the ground under other circumstances, totally unrelated to the church, because if there was anything my father hated it was "a chicken-eating preacher." It was well understood that my mother married my father over the objections of her family, first of all her father.

My father had no patience at all with churchgoing. If you asked him, he'd tell you in a minute, "No. There ain't no God. And I'm the only Santa Claus you ever gonna see."

Mother was different. Proverbs, parables, and principles poured out of her mouth in a constant stream. She had a quotation to fit every occasion, chief among them was, "Honor thy father and thy mother, that thy days may be long upon this earth."

When I hassled her in the kitchen as she prepared a meal, singing what came to be my song—"I'm huuuunnngrrryy!!"—Mother would retort, "Run around the house and catch Congry." Which would send me into spasms of frustrated rage.

"Get out of here, boy," she'd scat me. "Watch a pot and it'll never boil."

If her nose itched, mother would say, "Hmm! Nose itching. Company's coming." And someone was bound to show up.

She believed in God, dreams, luck, and intuition. Before she'd allow me to crawl into bed at night, I had to say my prayer, repeating it nightly down a misty string of years:

> Now I lay me down to sleep,
>   I pray the Lord my soul to keep.

> If I should die before I wake,
> I pray the Lord my soul to take.
>   Amen.

Being the oldest boy, I was the apple of my daddy's eye, which set me at irreconcilable odds with Helen and Wilhelmina. Not so much Helen as Wilhelmina, who was my active antagonist, my implacable foe. Being neither the oldest girl nor the oldest boy, Helen played the classic neutral, wishing a plague upon both our houses. With stony objectivity, she'd tell the pure truth on either of us if we lied about who hit whom first. The rub between Wilhelmina and me wasn't any lightweight sibling rivalry. It was closer to war. This was made forever clear to me one day when Wilhelmina, crying and fussing because she had to wash dishes, threw a fork—I had patted my fanny at her, all the while tautingly intoning, "Ha, ha, ha. You have to do the dishes"—which plunged deeply into my arm just as I ran out of the kitchen. For years thereafter, I wore the marks of the four prongs on my left forearm and remembered the incident as my first encounter with a witch.

Daddy had two jobs—waiting tables during the day in a big hotel restaurant, playing the piano in a club at night. We didn't see much of him; he was always either going or coming. When he was home, if he was not digging in the ground, he was sawing and nailing planks of wood, in a constant struggle to keep our house from collapsing. I liked helping him work, handing him the hammer or nails, or helping him shovel the dirt he dug up with the pick. Once I thought my daddy was magic. He drove the pick deep into the ground, and when he pulled it out there was a brand new penny stuck to the dirt clinging to one of the points of the pick. He gave me the penny. He repeated this magic feat five times, each time coming up with a brand new penny, giving it to me.

Daddy had a piano in a room of our house. We called it the Piano Room. Anybody who fooled around in the Piano Room was just begging for a whipping. The only person who could have her way in the Piano Room was Wilhelmina, whom Daddy was teaching how to play.

Mother had the uncanny ability to smell snakes. She said they smelled like watermelon rinds. One day she said some snakes were around somewhere close because she smelled them. Daddy said she was crazy, but agreed to have a look. He found two big black snakes under our house. He chopped off their heads and nailed their bodies to a tree stump in our backyard. They wiggled and thrashed around, seemingly more full of life without their heads than with them. Daddy said they'd keep it up until the sun went down, then they'd die. I watched them, glued to the spot, until mother made me come inside for dinner and bed. The next morning, I ran outside to see. The snakes were strangely stilled. I watched them for hours. Not a twitch.

Getting an education was a religion in our house. Mother was the high priestess of its doctrine. According to her, the worst thing in life was to miss an education. It was worse than going to Hell. It was Hell on earth. At least get a high school education! Later on, we'd need a high school diploma to get even the lowest job, like digging ditches. Mother never let up on this line—never—as she sought to instill in us the motivation to pursue education. She taught us how to read and gave us books for presents on birthdays and other occasions.

One day, suddenly, a dark shadow fell across our home. Daddy took an axe and chopped up his piano. Then he broke everything in the house made of glass, starting with all the dishes. He smashed the glass covers on the pictures hanging on the walls. One corner of our living room was like a family shrine, whose focus was my parents' wedding photo on the wall. Hanging around this photo, and on little whatnot shelves on either side, were our treasured family photos and memorabilia. Daddy smashed everything. Something terrible was happening. What it was I didn't know. Helen, Wilhelmina, Mother and Daddy all seemed to understand. But James, Theophilus, and I were told to shut up, get out of the room, or slapped when we demanded to know what was going on. We were never told.

After that, the fighting started. Every Saturday night, without fail, Daddy sarted beating Mother. There was screaming and the thunder of our feet and bodies scuffling around as we all joined in the melee. It was everybody against Daddy, and we'd all hit him as hard as we could, trying to make him stop hurting our mother. The center of my frustration was that I was unable to hit Daddy hard enough. That was the beginning of my driving ambition to hurry and grow up tall and strong, like my daddy, but bigger and stronger than he, so that I could beat him down to the ground the way he beat my mother.

I remember the comment C. P. Snow made in *Variety of Men* about the childhood of Joseph Stalin, comparing it to other revolutionary leaders—

> Nearly all the others came from professional families. Stalin alone was born in the depths of the poor. His father was not only an impoverished shoemaker, but an increasingly unsuccessful one. He took to vodka and to ill-treating his son. At a very early age Stalin had to reckon with savage brutality: he learned to be secretive, evasive, enduring, and to keep his mouth shut. It was an awful home, and he learned his lessons well.

One day Daddy said he was going far away and wasn't coming back. He was going to find us another house, in Chicago, Arizona, or California. Mother was getting fat in the belly and we were going to have a new house and a new baby in the family. Meanwhile, we were going to go live on

Grandpa Cleaver's farm. For my mother, moving onto the Cleaver farm in Wabbaseka was like going backwards, and my two sisters shared the same feeling. My two younger brothers were too young to know the difference, but for me it was a happy occasion. There were so many exciting things happening on the farm, so many worlds to explore.

Mother took a job teaching at the little school in the area, and she kept my two sisters with her all day. I had to go to school every afternoon, while one of the neighbor ladies kept James and Theophilus. I spent the rest of the time tagging behind Grandpa Cleaver as he did his daily chores. I'd help him feed the hogs and chickens, ride on the back of his horse-drawn wagon when he went to the company store. But my greatest pleasure was to take his dog, Shep, and go out hunting rabbits. When Shep spotted a rabbit, that rabbit was as good as in the pot. Shep would run it to the ground, grab it in his mouth, and shake it to death. Then he'd bring it back to me. Proudly, I'd run home with our catch. These were days of kissing the earth, of touching and smelling wild things growing, of running barefoot through cotton fields, of fishing in rivers and dragging in crawdad holes, of watching Grandpa and his friends slaughter hogs, of later sneaking in the smokehouse and licking the salty smoked hams hanging there. Thus I spent the time waiting for my father to send for us.

PHOENIX WAS SO HOT you saw heat waves steaming up from the earth. Running around barefoot was a perilous affair. Some nights the air inside our house was so heavy with heat we slept outside on the ground. There was nothing interesting about our new house. It was one in a row of cracker boxes and distinguishable only by its place in the line. There was no red clay in the back yard, no planted fields in which to chase rabbits with a dog. And the house sat so low to the ground you couldn't even crawl underneath to play games. From the back, you looked out across an empty space. Two hundred yards away was Buckeye Road.

Daddy called Buckeye Road "the bucket of blood." A long dirt road set apart from everything else, Buckeye Road was the local red-light district. It was reminiscent of the one main drag in a cowboy movie, and the action could have come from the same source. Whorehouses, gambling joints, and bars lined both sides of the road. After dark, especially on weekends, Buckeye Road would be all lit up, creating quite a spectacle to watch when we slept outside. Music blasted loudly from the jukeboxes, making you feel right there instead of a couple hundred yards away. People danced in the streets, shouted, laughed, talked loud, and whooped it up. Now and then, like a form of punctuation, a woman would scream. Once in a while shots rang out. Often we saw people fighting, ending with the blood-curdling whine of the ambulance siren.

Daddy had a job "running on the road," working as a waiter on trains. He was gone for weeks at a time, to Los

Angeles, San Francisco, or Chicago. When he came home, even though mother was getting bigger and bigger with the baby, the fighting continued. It was as though Buckeye Road walked across the vacant space and entered our house.

We arrived in Phoenix just before the beginning of summer vacation, 1945, but early enough to justify enrolling in school. On my first day in school, it was so hot in the classroom I barely held out until the final bell. The only thing I learned in that class was how to breathe hot air without fainting, which is what everybody else seemed to be studying, including the teacher. But in spite of the atrocious heat inside the classrooms, I loved going to school because it afforded access to the rough and tumble camaraderie of a large number of children my own age. When vacation finally rolled around, I had found my place amongst the boys in the neighborhood.

That summer in Phoenix, I found for the first time a place for myself outside our home. Nothing at home attracted me to stick around. I wanted to get as far away from my sisters and brothers as possible, and when Daddy came home, I wanted to be around as little as possible. Each morning I hit the streets at the same time as the sun, returning a little sad each evening at sundown.

Summer vacation was a festival without end. It was a time for having fun. I learned how to swim, box, play football, and run track; how to earn money shining shoes, and also how to steal watermelons and cantaloupes out of the boxcars down at the nearby train station.

I loved the camaraderie of the brotherhood constituted by the boys in the neighborhood. Within that larger horde, two boys, Felton and Otha, soon became my inseparable chums. We went everywhere together, enjoying every minute, and suffered whenever we had to part. Together, we gathered wood from packing crates and made ourselves shoeshine boxes, with straps on them for carrying over our shoulders. For reasons I didn't understand, it was best for us to stay out of the downtown area with our shoeshine boxes. If we got caught downtown by the police, a terrible fate lay in store for us.

But the best place for finding customers who wanted a shoeshine was downtown, and catching customers in the outlying areas was hard scratching. Inevitably, we were drawn into the forbidden downtown territory by the magnet of greater opportunity. With a little luck, we could catch a few customers and still have time either to go swimming or to the movies, all in the same day.

One day, Otha, Felton and I had penetrated deeply into downtown territory and were walking around trying to catch customers. Suddenly about five big burly white cops came from out of nowhere and swooped down upon us. In no time, they had confiscated our shine boxes, loaded us in the back seat of a patrol car, and sped away to the police station. We were terrified, not knowing really what to expect. The cops laid it on heavy about how big a crime we had committed. They let us know that we were in big trouble.

After our arrival at the police station, they locked us in a holding cell and kept us waiting for what seemed like an eternity. Finally, a cop came and unlocked the door, telling us to follow him. He led us to a big squad room, along one side of which was a large rack on which rested several shoeshine boxes, all of which were painted the same shade of blue with a round yellow/gold disc painted on either end. I had seen boys wandering around downtown with those shine boxes, and now I understood where they came from. Had there been any doubt, the cop soon swept it all away.

He explained to us that we were free to shine shoes in the downtown area any time, as long as we used one of

these blue and gold shine boxes. The boxes belonged to the
police. The fee was twenty-five cents a day, half that for
half a day. They supplied all the polish and saddlesoap
free. All we had to do was come in, check out a shine box,
go shine shoes, and bring the box back when we were
finished—dropping off the rental fee, of course. This
sounded like a good deal, the way the cop explained it, particularly since we would be free to ply our trade all over
the downtown area. An added boon was that we would be
free of the burden of dragging our shine boxes along with
us to the swimming pool or to the movie theater.

It turned out, however, that there was a great gap between the way the cop explained it and the way things
turned out. By the time we had earned enough money to
pay off the fee and to have enough for ourselves, it was
too late to go to the movies or to the swimming pool.
Everything was thrown out of rhythm. On top of that,
Daddy found out what I was doing and forbade me to do
it anymore. But the lure of the nickels and dimes turned
out to be stronger than my father's injunction. Besides,
he'd be gone out of town most of the time and so wouldn't
even know.

One day, I was downtown, down on my knees, putting
the finishing touches on a man's shoes when suddenly I
was snatched up by the nape of my neck. Shoe polish,
shinebox, rag, and shoe brush all went in different direc-
tions. It was Daddy. He told the protesting customer to go
to hell and me to head for home, slapping me on the head
every few steps. I tried to explain to him that the cops
were going to be mad if I didn't show up with their
twenty-five cents and their shine box. At that, he demanded
that I give him the cops' twenty-five cents. He took it and
threw it out in the middle of the street, saying that if they
wanted it they could get down on their knees and pick it
up. Then he gave me a stern warning, that if he ever caught

me shining shoes again, he'd break my neck. I believed him, and to this day I've never looked upon shining shoes as one of the choices open to me.

"Ain't no son of mine gonna shine no damn shoes!" Daddy said, slapping me behind the head again to underline his point.

Swimming. I took to water like a fish. I had never even heard of swimming before coming to Phoenix. Now I was going swimming every day. Swimming came easy to me, and soon I was participating in the contests which were held each week. My proudest moment came the day I won a red ribbon for coming in first. I was as proud as a member of the Hall of Fame even though I had just won a race between beginners.

Boxing. We'd go down to the boxing arena which we called Madison Square Garden. The older boys gave us boxing lessons. We'd dress up just like big boxers, put on boxing gloves just like theirs. They taught us how to block punches, jab, and connect with a strong right hand. Soon we were putting on exhibitions between fights once each week, to the delight of the crowds that screamed for blood.

Stealing. Watermelons, cantaloupes, and other fruits and vegetables were shipped by train through Phoenix. On any given day, hundreds of boxcars heavily laden with such goodies passed through the train station in a monotonous convoy. We'd sneak up into the staging areas of the train yard, pick the type of fruit or melons we wanted today, then eat until our bellies about popped open. My favorite was watermelon. I enjoyed popping one open, devouring its heart, and throwing the rest away. Then I'd start on another one. I'd polish off five or six big watermelons at each sitting.

The approach of my birthday kicked off a crisis in my family. I was absolutely determined to have a pair of drapes to wear. Mother was dead set against it on the grounds that I was too young. But all my friends either already had a pair or were going to get some soon. Until then, I always wore distinctively "little boy's" clothes. Now I was ready for a change of life. All my friends were ready for it too. Not to get a pair of drapes out of my birthday seemed to me to be about the worst thing that could happen to a boy. As August 31 approached, I escalated my entreaties and complaints. But Mother was adamant. According to her, I was just a baby boy acting too old for his britches. Each time she said "No!" it bruised my heart and soul. It was with the most profound anxiety that on my birthday I started opening up the boxes containing my presents. In a big box marked to me from my sister Wilhelmina, I found what I was looking for: a blue suit with drape-legs on the pants. It was my first experience with forgive and forget. I put on my drape suit and walked up and down the sidewalk all day, showing myself in the full pride of a boy no longer too young, a young man coming into being.

Suddenly summer was over. The party ended. It was back to school again. Time was flying. Mother went away to the hospital. She came back days later with a baby girl named Claudette, born December 4, 1945. Now my family was even: there were three girls and three boys. But that didn't stop Daddy from starting fights with Mommy. In fact, the pace of the confrontations seemed to increase, the bitterness of the strife intensified. Daddy even got upset and angry over whether or not Claudette looked like him. It was war as usual.

One day I was playing marbles with the gang. It was a hotly contested affair. Suddenly there was a great commotion. I looked up in time to see my mother run by screaming, followed a few seconds later by my father. They were at it again. I felt deeply humiliated before this jury of my peers. I scrambled to my feet and took off in the direction of my parents, to help my mother, and already tensing up to hit my father with all my might.

Then one day Mommy and Daddy announced that we were moving. We were leaving Phoenix, Arizona, for good. We were California-bound. In California, the streets were made of gold. Orange trees grew wild everywhere, and Hollywood, home and source of the movies, was located in the Golden State. I was ready to go. Sweet as Phoenix had been, with the boxing, swimming, and free watermelons, it was not the stuff of my dreams. California, on the other hand, fired my imagination. There was magic in its legend, power in its name. California, here I come.

3

CALIFORNIA
CHOICES

THERE ACTUALLY WERE orange trees in California, but I am
unable to determine whether the oranges in my memory
were hanging on the trees I saw upon arriving in Los
Angeles on the train from Phoenix one bright sunny day.
From Little Rock, we had traveled West as far as we could
go, to the edge of the continent, and now we had run out
of land. This had to be home because there was no place
else to go, except backwards.

Daddy had chosen Los Angeles as a function of the rail-
roads. He had landed a new job as waiter on the Super
Chief, running from Los Angeles to Chicago, of which he
was very proud. But it had cost him a fortune to get us all

to California intact, what with the new baby and all. So we were barely able to make ends meet.

Houses were scarce because of discriminatory practices, so there were not enough to fill the needs of the thousands of blacks migrating to California from the South in pursuit of job opportunities tossed up by the War. We had two rooms in a large house on Newton Street, just off Central Avenue on the East Side. The house sat across from Newton Street Police Station, which added a certain amount of drama to our lives, as there was always a lot of hustle and bustle going on there. There was no way to determine how many people lived in our house. The house was run by a lady named Gladys, and people used to sleep there in shifts. How anybody slept there I don't know, because I hardly could. There was too much coming and going. On top of that, the record player was kept going at full blast. There was a whole lot of fussing and fighting. The turnover was quick, and people only stayed there long enough to get something better together.

The turnover was quick for everybody except us. We seemed to be settling in. Wilhelmina, Helen, and I were enrolled in school. My school was right around the corner from the house. The first day I went there the other kids poked fun at me, allowing as how I was fresh out of the woods. They laughed at my country boy haircut: I wore bangs, a hairstyle popular among blacks in the South in those days. The hair in the front was allowed to grow as long as it would and the rest was cut as short as you could. Then the front was packed with grease and combed back over one's peel head. The kids laughed at me because they had been laughed at in their turn, just as I would later laugh at the new country kids who came after me.

The kids also laughed at my Southern accent. This reached its peak one day when I said something about "way over yonder." That's when the fighting began. Now the circle was complete. There was fighting at home, fighting in Gladys's house all around us, fighting up and down the street, and fighting at school. Lucky for me I had learned something about boxing; it stood me in good stead. But fighting in the ring was different from fighting after school. Boxing had its limits. You knew where you stood. There was a beginning and an end, and you could call it quits whenever you wanted to. Not so when fighting after school. The other kids seemed intent upon either bloodying your nose or making you cry. One or the other. They would even kick you if you went down.

At first I tried to skirt past these fights, and I would run straight home when school was out. But the other kids would have none of that. Finally they cornered me, and so I had to go for what I knew. What I knew was not enough to win but just enough to gain a little respect. Although they made my nose bleed, my pride was that I did not cry, and I made their noses bleed too. And since new kids were arriving all the time, I soon became a part of the campus regulars and did my part in putting vamp on the new arrivals.

Central Avenue reminded me of Buckeye Road in Phoenix, except that whereas Buckeye Road was set off to the side, and you could avoid it if you chose, there was no getting around Central Avenue. It was the main drag, the artery, the lifeline of black Los Angeles. At that time, black people in Los Angeles were confined almost exclusively to the east side, packed in on top of each other. Born of the prosperity that grew out of the War, and animated by the spirit of Live Today For Tomorrow We May Die, Central Avenue boasted a booming nightlife. It was dancing, gambling, and cut 'n' shoot; pimping, whoring, and get rich quick. On weekends we'd go to the movies, to the Lincoln and Rose Bud theaters. And we did a lot of just walking up and down Central Avenue, like everybody else did, looking at each other, in that way making something out of nothing.

Finally, our turn came to move out of Gladys's house. Daddy had gotten back on his financial feet. He found us a house of our own—"as far away from all these niggers as we can get," is how he put it. Mother, Wilhelmina, and Helen didn't like it one bit. They were happy to live on the East Side, especially Wilhelmina. She had found herself a job at the Club Alabam, was moving with a fast crowd, and didn't want to hear anything about moving out into the woods. And Mother wanted to stay near Aunt Ozel and all their friends. And Helen wanted to stay so she could attend Jefferson High School. But Daddy swept all of their arguments aside. Piling our belongings in the back of a truck, he said, "Come on. We're moving to Rose Hill!"

Rose Hill was the closest thing to Wabbaseka we had seen since leaving Arkansas. Located near the foothills of Pasadena, surrounded by Eagle Rock, Alhambra, El Sereno, and Lincoln Heights, Rose Hill didn't feature on anybody's map. Once it had been an exclusively Chicano neighborhood (neighborhood in the grand sense of the word). There is something deeply tribal in the Chicano sense of community, held together by a fierce loyalty as thick as blood. Rose Hill had been one of these old, proud Chicano communities, like Mara, Happy Valley, Alpine, and so on. Traditionally, it had boasted one of the fiercest gangs in Los Angeles. During the war years and the aftermath, Rose Hill was one of the bastions of the Pachuco culture.

Our arrival in Rose Hill was viewed by old-timers as part of the disintegration of the old neighborhood, part of the destruction of the Chicano culture and cohesive community. There were in fact three Rose Hills, superimposed upon each other and blending together with great difficulty and pain.

First there was the old Chicano layer, dating back in time as far as one cared to go. These were the original people, great extended families and clans, who always were there. These families had built their own homes on the naked roads, at a time when there were no roads, electricity, running water, or any of the other amenities of an urban settlement. Their relationship with the rest of Los Angeles was purely theoretical, and they liked it that way.

But with the explosion of Los Angeles' population during the War, there had been a steady encroachment upon their community, as part of that great wave of humanity spilled over the edge of the city proper. In coming to terms with this population explosion, Los Angeles invoked powers of eminent domain, by which the heart of Old Rose Hill was extirpated in one fell swoop. The neighborhood was literally gutted, and the population removed in a messy, scandal-ridden resettlement scheme that was one of the greatest land-grab rip-offs of all times.

Once the core of the population was driven out of their houses, bulldozers were hastily sent in to demolish them to insure that no matter what the outcome of the litigation in the courts instigated by the displaced population, they would never return to their homes because their homes were no more. As a clincher, a low-cost housing project was constructed capable of housing several hundred families. The people who were moved into this housing project bore no relationship to the Rose Hill of old, and were there only because their names had popped up on a beaureaucrat's waiting list down at the Housing Authority. Most of the newcomers were hardship cases, at a time when welfare and public assistance was considered immoral. They were mostly wives of servicemen living off allotments, or divorcees living off alimony. Here and there were whole stable families, but this was very rare. So these people, who constituted the second Rose Hill, were disliked and

resented by the hill people, the remaining original in-
habitants.

My family was part of the third layer of the population.
After gutting the old Rose Hill and erecting the housing
project, the city fathers seemed to have abandoned their
master plan for the area. All new construction was halted.
The bulldozers were withdrawn. Grass and weeds quickly
overran the excavated construction sites. Great controver-
sies raged in courts and in the chambers of commerce and
councils of government. But the people of Rose Hill were
unrepresented and were left to rumor, fear, and confusion.
Land speculators were active. They came in posing as government officials and bought up all the houses they could
from the old-timers, then rented them out to the house-
hungry throngs pouring into California from every state
in the Union. Daddy had found such a house. He considered that he had struck a good bargain. The migration
of our family had ended. Rose Hill became, in that sacred
sense of roots and soil and soul, Home.

THE HOUSE WE MOVED into belonged to the church standing twenty yards away, and both the house and the church belonged to Elder Richardson. Elder Richardson was an enterprising old preacher from East Los Angeles who had taken an old building, renovated it, and set up a church, hoping to fashion a congregation out of the increasing number of black families moving to Rose Hill. Since we lived in his house, Elder Richardson fully expected our family to set an example by regularly attending his services.

On our first Sunday in the new house, the whole family, except my father, turned out for services. Daddy's absence didn't go unnoticed by Elder Richardson. Mother had urged him to come, if for no other reason than to make a good first impression in our new community. But Daddy brushed the idea aside impatiently.

"I ain't got no time for that foolishness," he said.

To attract people to the services, Elder Richardson had a man stand out in front of the church with a set of drums, beating them so loudly they could be heard for a mile. The whole area consisted of rolling hills, and the sound of the drums bounced back and forth off the hills in colliding echoes. Each Sunday morning, the whole neighborhood got startled to attention by the boom, boom, boom of the big bass drum. Daddy couldn't stand it. When he was home, he liked to sleep late on Sunday. The first few times it happened, he let it go with a lot of grumbling. But finally, one Sunday morning, he went outside and made the man stop beating the drums.

"Take that racket away from here, buddy," he said, "or I'll wrap those drums around your head!"

After that, it was a state of war between Daddy and Elder Richardson. Elder Richardson was an old man, brown-skinned, with a smooth head almost totally bald. There was a little fringe of white hair around the edges, running from his temples back over his ears to the nape of his neck. He had a set of even, sparkling white false teeth, and he looked like a pious, God-fearing old man. I was always amazed at the way Daddy talked about Elder Richardson, with an aggressive hatred for preachers in general. It must have come from some grudge carried away from his own father. For his part, Elder Richardson used to single out Daddy as a perfect example of an unfit, uncouth, sinful, country nigger who was destined to come to no good, and who was jeopardizing the souls of his children. More than once he asked the congregation to say a special prayer for the Cleavers.

One day, the house at the top of the hill caught on fire. By the time the fire department and the neighbors put out the flames, the entire roof had been destroyed. The house belonged to an old white lady known as Mary Goat, who derived her name from the strong odor she emitted from the multiple layers of sweaters, skirts, and coats which she wore winter, summer, and fall. Mary Goat had rented the house to a large clan of black people from Tennessee, the Grandisons, whose pride was a huge ten-wheel army truck in which they had driven all the way from Nashville to Los Angeles.

Mary Goat had the reputation of being very rich, a rumor fed by the fact that, periodically, she could be seen passing by in a huge chauffeur-driven limousine. At other times, she'd be seen walking by leaning on a gnarled walking cane, followed by several dogs and the odor for which she was named. When the house burned, the Grandisons piled their belongings in their army truck and moved to another house on the other side of the hill.

Daddy saw opportunity. He caught up with Mary Goat

as she poked around in the ashes and rubble of her house
and offered to buy it from her. Mary Goat snapped up the
cash down payment Daddy offered. Daddy was alone in the
enthusiasm he showed for the deal he had made.

For the next few months, Daddy spent every spare moment he could find working on the burnt-out house. He
paid no attention to the protests of my mother. He'd paint
a glowing picture in words of how great that house was
going to be some day. To top it off, he said, he was going to
build a stairway out of unhewn logs with a gate and arch-
way at the edge of our lot, just at the point where the level
ground on which the house stood dropped down sharply
for about ten feet.

As soon as the house was all cleaned up and the roof
almost complete, Daddy couldn't wait until it was all
finished. He insisted that we move in right away. Mother
refused. There was a big fight. Mother took the three girls
and split, leaving me and my two brothers with my father.
We moved out of Elder Richardson's house into our new
house farther up the hill.

No sooner were we in than it started raining real hard.
It must have rained forty days and forty nights. At any
rate, it was too much for the repairs which my father had
made on the burnt-out roof. I remember seeing my father,
one night, crying his heart out as he held an umbrella over
me and my two brothers as we tried to sleep under the
leaky roof through which the rain poured like a sieve.

We survived the rains. Daddy finished the work on the
roof. We now owned our own six-room house. Mother
came back with the three girls. Daddy went to work on
the yard. He laid out a plan. Every day after school, I was
required to come home and work for one hour with the
pick and shovel, leveling off and extending the yard. Finally, the day came when Daddy completed the stairway
and arch made out of unhewn logs. Many a day I watched

him when he came home from work. He'd pause at the bottom of the hill and look up at that arch. Then he'd make his way slowly, but proudly, up the hill.

One day Elder Richardson and another man came up to our stairs and started chopping them down with axes. In a few moments they demolished what it had taken Daddy months to construct. Elder Richardson said that the stairs were on his property, that our property ended at the embankment.

"Why didn't you say something before the stairs were finished?" Mother asked him.

"I ain't got to say anything if I don't want to," Elder Richardson said.

"Elder Richardson," my mother said, "I think you just made a big mistake."

I was sitting on the edge of the embankment, anxiously awaiting my father that evening. He always came home at just about the same time. But this evening it seemed like he would never show. Finally, in the distance, I saw him coming. As always, he stopped at the bottom of the hill and looked up. But this time he just stood in one spot for a very long time, as though he could not believe his eyes. He walked slowly up the hill, slower than usual. He paused at the bottom of the embankment, standing amongst the ruins of his stairway, looking his silent question up into my eyes.

"Elder Richardson and another man did it," I said. "Elder Richardson said that's his property down there. They chopped it down with axes."

Daddy looked around him in helpless disbelief. Slowly, silently, he walked around to where the embankment was lowest and climbed up into the yard. "Well, I'll be damned," he finally said.

That Sunday, when the drums started booming down at the bottom of the hill, calling the people to come to church, we were all sitting around watching Daddy. He didn't stay in bed late like he usually did on Sunday. Instead, he was up early, fully dressed, and waiting. Now he stood up. He had a hammer in his hand. Mother tried to stop him, tried to bar the door, but he wouldn't listen. We followed him down the hill. He walked up to the man beating the drums and started hitting him with the hammer. He kicked and stomped the drums to pieces. Then he went inside the church. Elder Richardson was standing in front of the altar, the Bible spread out before him, looking peaceful and pious as usual. Daddy walked up and hit that old man on the head with the hammer, and then started smashing up everything in sight. The people ran outside, Elder Richardson foremost amongst them. There was blood pouring from an ugly cut in his skull. I remember watching Daddy very deliberately take Elder Richardson's false teeth, which had fallen out of his mouth, and smash them to bits with the hammer.

The cops came and took Daddy away. But later on that day, he came back home. He fixed the stairway again. And this time nobody knocked it down. Elder Richardson never held services in that church again. We took the church and turned it into sort of a clubhouse. Over the years, it was completely destroyed. But little by little.

SOMETHING ABOUT living in Rose Hill forced one to choose between two worlds—the world of the Chicanos, La Raza; and the world of the *myates*, or the blacks, which was perceived as an appendage of the official white world. Language drew the line between the two worlds, marking an allegiance to a spirit of opposition to the white man's world. The supreme embodiment of the Chicano as implacable foe of the dominant white culture was the Pachuco, the generic label for young Chicanos whose life style was defiance of and resistance to the official white programs and culture. The strong fortress of the Chicanos was their language, which could be penetrated but not conquered. The Pachucos were cultural heroes—warriors who pitted their pride and defiance against overwhelming odds.

The Pachucos loomed larger than life. Each Chicano neighborhood had its gang of Pachucos. The Pachucos asked no quarter and were given none. The very name *Pachuco* was a synonym for violence and death. On the one hand the cops waged war against all Pachucos, and on the other, the Pachucos waged war against each other. Each neighborhood was a sacred turf, and the Pachucos often killed each other on sight, with no words spoken, for no other reason than the victim's being a stranger caught on another gang's land.

Not all Chicanos were Pachucos; that would have been too heavy! But there was something of the Pachuco in every Chicano. The Pachucos let their hair grow long, combing it in a distinctive style called the duck tail. They wore zoot suits and shiny shoes and carried razors, knives, and guns. Each Pachuco stood on his own reputation. Reputation was an active category, and one had to have exploits to one's credit, scalps to display, to add content and luster to one's name. Strength was admired and life was a trial by fire. Insult or injury could only be met by retaliation and revenge. The vendetta was the way of life.

The day of the Pachuco was on the wane by the time my family moved to Rose Hill. Those who remained were the last of the Mohicans, so to speak. Like all cultural heroes riding the wave of the future, the Pachucos staked out new territory for their people. A violent explosion, the Pachuco phenomenon gave rise to myth, and a generation of Chicanos recounted their exploits. Proclaiming their glory, they carved their names on trees, wrote them with in-eradicable dyes and inks on walls of buildings. The mono-graphs and slogans which they left behind were constant reminders to others that great warriors of pride had passed this way.

I stood in awe of the Pachucos and never tired of hear-ing of their exploits. That something wild about them spoke to something wild in me. I made friends quickly and easily with the Chicano boys my age, and the Spanish they spoke came easily also. The simple fact was that they had more freedom from family restraint than the black boys had, at a time when I was beginning to break away from the controls of my home.

The starting point was that when darkness began to fall, my little black friends had to rush home. If they stayed out too late, they faced the wrath of their fathers. My father also laid down strict orders to me to be home no later than 8:00 P.M. We'd all hang out together till the last minute; then one by one we'd drift towards the pad, the order of going depending upon the amount of parental restraint we were under. I was always the last black cat to split, and the Chicanos used to laugh at us, calling us mommy's boys and scaredy-cats.

My struggle with my father, to break his power over me, centered on the question of whether or not I kept the deadline which he set upon me. Every night, I'd come home late. And every night my father would beat me. As time went by, the beatings became more severe. At the same time, I was growing bigger and stronger, and the beatings began to hurt me less and less. My feelings, my pride, my sense of dignity and worth suffered more than I did physically. Seeing this, my father increased the violence of his attacks in an effort to break me down.

The fact that my father was fighting with me didn't stop the fights he'd start with my mother. But where he and I would go round in circles every night, Saturday nights were set aside for the main event between him and Mother. It was in this atmosphere that I slowly began to conceive the idea of killing my father. It seemed the logical, inevitable conclusion of the collision course we were on.

One night, I came home late as usual. Daddy was waiting for me when I entered the door. Without saying a word to me, he started hitting me with a stick. I grabbed hold of the stick and wouldn't let go. He tried with all his might to wrest the stick free, but couldn't. In the past, I had never hit my father back when he was beating me. But during his fights with my mother, I'd hit him as hard as I could. This night, I let go with my right hand and hit Daddy a staggering blow in his chest. I could feel the strength seep out of him as he stumbled backwards. He recovered, breathing with great difficulty, and then flew into a rage. He raised the stick and came down again and again upon my head. As I lost consciousness, I heard my sister Wilhelmina screaming at him to stop before he killed me.

Up in the hills, there was a house built in a tree that we

used to play in. The next night, I decided that I wouldn't go home at all. Instead, I, along with a couple of my little Chicano friends, spent the night in the tree house, knowing full well that it would bring my conflict with my father to a head. I had a knife and had locked my mind on the idea that when my father hit me again, I was going to plunge it into his heart. I knew that I would do it. Everything had been building to this point. I was ready.

As usual, my father went to work early that morning, and I came home after he left, cleaned myself up, and went to school. All day long I was thinking about what would happen that night. I looked forward to it with a wild anticipation, eager to get it over with.

That night, I came home late, the open knife in my pocket, clutched and ready in my hand. I took a deep breath as I entered the door, thinking to myself, *This is it*. Daddy was sitting in a chair looking at me. He didn't speak, nor did he make a move towards me. I stood there for a minute, waiting for him to leap to his feet and go into his act. But he didn't move. Finally, he spoke. "Go on to bed," he said. "Go on to bed." Never again did he raise his hand against me. Nor did he hit my mother again. Instead, he disappeared, went away. It was five years before I saw him again.

The nine years that I spent in prison (San Quentin, Folsom, California Men's Colony East, and Soledad, again) were the transition days that took me from marijuana-peddling rapist to revolutionary. I would go the whole route of being enamored with Marxism, initiated in the Black Muslim religion, and of reading the Great Books. Frankly, the study of the Great Books did more for me intellectually than the other two. The Black Panther Party, which I joined upon my release from prison, was to become the political and social vehicle for the ideas that captured my attention.

4

3,285 DAYS
EQUALS PRISON

THE PLAY-ACTING OF the criminal is hourly theater. When, in my late teens, I started to develop the rape routine in the motel circuit, I usually posed as an investigative agent or private detective coming to question a couple in their room. After tying up the man, I first would look at their I.D. cards, check out who they were, and quickly discover that they were not husband and wife. I'd act like I was writing this information down on a pad, creating a scene that would plague their operative paranoia in whatever they were into or shouldn't have been into. They wouldn't dare report me as I had masqueraded as some off-balance investigator. All the crime shows on television played into my act.

The returns on this two-month sexual assault, shake-down period were not much beyond the ego power they seemed to offer. The sense of manipulation, rage and madness, all which infect the criminal mind, must be dramatically and lastingly changed if real amendment of life is to happen. I believe nothing short of Christian conversion can truly reshape and redirect the professional gangster. In their book, *The Criminal Personality,** Dr. Samuel Yochelson and Dr. Stanton E. Samenow don't mince words about the process: a "total destruction of the criminal's personality" is required. That may sound like a heavy trip; but a light one of the kind going on in so many institutions today simply will not work. My personality change took a long and tortuous path. Prison gave me some fresh expressions for my rage and madness, also some new cunning that would permit me the time at last to reach a mature confrontation with myself and the bankruptcy of the several lives that I had tried to fashion and which failed.

In my intensive outlaw period, I always felt that I had a short time left on earth. I lived constantly under the gun and with my gun, always believing that I would be blown away at any moment. And this was reality for my friends who went into armed robbery and were getting killed one after another in shoot-outs with the cops. Other acquaintances were overdosing with drugs. The ranks were thinning out swiftly. And in the high-powered, high-risk narcotic circuit, it was a constant struggle to keep from being eliminated, so one ended up eliminating people, and the death cycle was one big rip-off syndrome. Life became an open-ended thing where you could not permit yourself long-range plans; you lived day to day, wondering if you would make it 'til evening.

---

* New York: Aronson, 1976.

The criminal life is a double, triple exposure. Your family sort of guesses what you are into but are terrified to probe. One girlfriend in those years actually knew nothing about my outlaw existence, putting my occupation down as "hustling," a convenient, all-purpose term. Another companion was quite informed about my income arrangements and seemed terribly attracted to the danger, outlawry, and rip-off that made up my success as a drug dealer. Perhaps she marveled that I seemed so free, uncontrolled, and antiestablishment. I didn't have to go along with the system, a well-heeled, cocky rebel. Big and dangerous and rich—all the crowning symbols of the ghetto world were mine. Yet they were sustained by the elemental forces of destruction, and only when the full power of God through Christ began to enter my low existence as a fugitive in France was I able, at last, to conquer these ultimate enemies. God hates sin but not the sinner, and the demolition of evil works came out of Christ's love, which opened to me a present worth claiming and a future worth pursuing. Praise God for His salvation, which is powerful and personal and life-changing!

SINCE I COVERED SO much of the Black Muslim routine in *Soul on Ice* and my deep attachment to the personality and teachings of Malcolm X, it is important here to discuss some topics that I purposely avoided in that first book. Prison psychiatry is one. By far my most harrowing experience was with the shrinks and what they were trying to do to Negroes on the inside. But when one is still serving time, it doesn't advance the hours to reveal the awful truth about penal practices.

My situation was a living illustration of what Drs. Yochelson and Samenow talk about in *The Criminal Personality:* "A criminal is most vulnerable to change when he is locked up or is about to face a period of confinement, when his options in life are considerably reduced and he is more likely to reflect on his past." They go on to say that the criminal is faced with three remaining options: crime, suicide, or change. I temporarily added another option—going crazy. Here is what happened.

In prison everyone seems to have a particular outlet. Some jump right into the homosexual trip and spend their hours figuring out how to be with their sweetheart. Others make the prison scene an extension of their gang-life on the outside and invest energy and scheming on how to take over the place or at least run the rest of the yard in a threatening, intimidating, shakedown manner. Some become hustlers or full-time gamblers. Everyone tries occasional attempts at smuggling or undercover adventures. Religion is big with some. I eventually went into the world of ideas, literature, reading, and study—quite a contrast for a big, hulking drug-dealer. For a period I even took up the saxophone but discovered that I could not keep that going and sustain my study-writing interest. I finally opted for words.

But not before I had a long running battle with myself and the psychiatric staff of the prison. As I mentioned, in the early weeks that launched this major prison sentence I went off the deep end. I had managed to get hold of some mace (a spice used in cooking). The people I knew who took mace said that it was a real upper, that it made you feel like you were floating right over the wall. Often cellmates would take it just before they were going into some vigorous athletic event; they felt full of terrific energy and sought the high feeling that it generated. For a few packs of cigarettes, I had purchased a matchbox full of mace. You were supposed to take this kicker in the morning, so that by afternoon break you could be out in the exercise yard for your ups, wheeling and whirling around in some sort of unbridled ecstasy. Then by lockup time in the evening you would feel relaxed and tired and go to sleep easily.

My problem began by my taking the stuff at the wrong time of day—the afternoon. I had put my order in the day before, and should have received it that morning. Being contraband, it was dangerous stuff to keep on you. One wanted to receive it and swallow it in the same motion, in rapid sequence. Possession was a serious bust. So I immediately downed the spice with a big glass of hot water.

My dosage didn't take effect right away, not until early evening just as we were locked up. Then the sensations started to throb. Instead of being outside in the freedom and air of the exercise yard, I was jumping around in a tiny cell, my heart pounding, racing out of control. I was terrified. I thought I was having a heart attack. After several hours of pacing, I knew that I could no longer remain in that cell. I had to come out. I told the guard that I had to come out. I might as well have said that I wanted to go for a walk, a real no-no.

At night the keys to the cells and the cell block are taken clear outside the wall. A special security measure—no keys at night in the prison. I started banging on the door with my shoe, screaming to get out. The nearest guard asked what was wrong, and I said my heart. He said go to the hospital in the morning—take sick-call. There was no way that I could stay in that closet until morning. I started pounding and yelling until my friends woke up, and they supported my plea.

Eventually the guards went outside, got the keys, and unlocked my cell. The guards were angry. They yanked me out of the cell and said, "Well, what's wrong?" Anyone could see that my heart was racing, but they were wise and suspected drugs.

I took a look at all the white faces surrounding me. The guards, the people running the hospital, all of them were white. Mine was the only black face there. They would be looking at my eyes, listening to my chest. The only choice in this box was to feign irrational behavior, since they already had me down for possession of marijuana, and I definitely did not want the label of being a narco. Having a drug report laid on my already heavy sentence would be like compounding interest on my account, only it would have to be paid in the coin of months and years.

I started yelling about racism in the jail, about a white conspiracy to keep blacks down. The white guards and hospital attendants freaked out, panicked, and locked me up in a padded cell. By that time I had really bugged out. One attendant took notes, wrote down all my attacks on the white race and their oppression of Negroes. When Monday morning came, I was on the psychiatrist's list. He came and got me, so I had to go through with this act or fall back into a definite drug indictment, which my record could not stand.

There followed months and months of psychiatric questioning and counsel, during which I found myself in the clutches of some dangerous doctors. I even had group therapy, but the main round was between the shrink and myself. He eventually concluded that I hated my mother. I think, after I got to talking to him, I did express my true feelings; but I never understood why he said I hated my mother, because it wasn't true. Father hate, yes: I wanted to get him for years for what he did to me, my mother, and my family. But not my mother. This same physician, many years later, was sent to prison himself for declaring a man insane (in collusion with the man's wife) and then proceeding to take over his property.

The head of the department, a Dr. Schmidt, somewhere along the line had decided that Black Muslims were crazy, and the only way to straighten them out was through electric shock treatment. Sort of an American Eichmann or Himmler, he recommended shock every time he saw me, and he cooked the minds of some close friends—one a guy we called Turk and another, Brother Albert, both Muslim brothers. I had known Turk way back at age twelve or thirteen at Whittier. Both were shocked by Schmidt at San Quentin. Turk had been a real tough, aggressive person; after they shocked him, he was scared of his own shadow. Albert was the same way. Neither one got their brains or balance back. You could walk up to Albert and take his whole lunch tray away and he wouldn't say a thing or make a move. It was pathetic.

Of course, not all the medical profession in jail are weird or wacky. Later, when I was serving time in San Quentin I was put under the care of Dr. Alvin Carr, a white psychiatrist who helped me sort out many problems in my life. In individual counseling, we talked hundreds of hours, it seems, and he helped me through a very difficult period. He was a first-rate professional.

WHAT KEPT ME GOING in the early days of that nine-year stretch was the solidarity and brotherhood of the Black Muslims. My initial contact came through the prison hospital, where I had access to the mimeograph machine.

During the early sixties, Elijah Muhammad gained a substantial nationwide following. Many of his followers pursued their religious loyalty after they were imprisoned, and the movement really bloomed at Folsom and San Quentin. One strategy for Elijah was to take out paid advertisements in the *Los Angeles Herald Dispatch*, setting forth his principles and editorializing on the oppressive white devils. His column was clipped and passed along to me, and I would cut the stencil for a newsletter widely circulated behind bars. While the column was banned inside, it never failed to circulate a day after it appeared in the *Herald*.

While I never felt comfortable with Elijah's heaviest doctrine—the antagonism and hatred of the white devils—I did feel that it was effective in building solidarity and black awareness. The more I typed, the more I liked what I read. Elijah was building self-esteem into the lives of the lowest blacks. To those locked up, he gave dignity, belonging, and a cause; and we finally became the most singularly powerful group in the California prisons.

The Muslim message also took dead aim at a host of other evils that were destroying the family. Elijah stated that the drug-running—the pills, the grass, the heroin-shooting, as well as the Saturday night drinking brawls—had to stop. It was another way, he said, that the white devils were keeping us under their control—burning us out on the stuff and sticking us in prison when it got too absurd. Either way, the blacks were losers, and these became absolute doctrine: no more running, taking, or promoting drugs.

The Black Panthers benefited from the Muslim teaching —it would later become dogma for us as well, and probably saved us from total destruction. Of all the charges the cops piled upon us, that was one that never stuck because we were absolutely out of it. We ultimately got to the point where, in many urban ghetto neighborhoods, we shoved the drug syndicate clear out of the community. The hoods were looking straight down our gun barrels when they trucked that material into our towns. We said, "Show up once more with that stuff, and you are zero." They got the message, and so did the people in prison. The drug-free life for many prisoners began inside the slammer. And it was a powerful witness to the Muslim faith.

During those years of metamorphosis from reckless criminal to respected leader in the black community, I closely modeled my thinking and action after Malcolm X. He was the heir apparent of Elijah Muhammad and the prime minister of the movement. His style, fearlessness, and mental prowess gave us a hero to worship and follow. Like me, he had been a gangster (in Chicago), ruthless and gun-toting. He also encouraged the technique of analysis and brought this to play in pulling off the layers of white racism and oppression. He was well read, traveled a lot, and always seemed to have whitey on the defensive. The people in charge, the whites in America, were afraid of him. The Uncle Toms and boot-licking Negro leaders were stunned by Malcolm's audacity. When President Kennedy was assassinated, Malcolm's statement that "the chickens had come home to roost," proved his undoing. But most of the time he was right. American violence was homemade like apple pie, and Malcolm called the changes before your eyes.

Malcolm was more than a folk hero—he was the living sign of the future for thousands and thousands of blacks. Increasingly, Elijah and his inner circle became uncomfortable with the hard line that the heir apparent was taking. Before he knew what happened, for information was next to slow as far as the prisons went, Elijah publicly censured and silenced Malcolm and then expelled him from the movement. People on the conservative side of Elijah, if that was possible, put Malcolm down for his Kennedy chicken-roosting statement. They seemed to have been waiting for an opportunity to cut him down, and his remarks provided the ideal moment.

Other forces seemed to be building at this hour for a big split among the Muslims. (I was also in the center of these splits—first among the Muslims, and later in the division of the Panther Party. And when you split, things don't always multiply, sometimes they divide and fade.) Those who maneuvered the suspension of Malcolm X were propping up Elijah, so he was making these public statements in an Arizona health resort. He was quite old, and his true health condition was kept a complete secret, in somewhat the same way the Chinese started using Mao in his final months. These old men sit around in overstuffed chairs, drooling and staring straight ahead while the press releases churn with profound statements and revolutionary orders to be carried out.

The power scramble among Elijah's successors obviously no longer included Malcolm. The ideological disagreements were towering. Malcolm and people like myself were to become the militant force in the Muslim arena. Malcolm was all politics and economics, something that was practical and visible. Elijah—he loved to theologize. His teachings boiled in and out of the Bible, were a mishmash of Islam, incense, and nonsense. But his fiery convictions and enormous spiritual blueprint for black survival was compelling. Yet Malcolm was the realist to follow and eventually to fight for. When I announced for him in prison, it was like bringing the news of another California earthquake. I was met with stony silence and icy stares from most of the Muslim loyalists. They believed Elijah. Only when the pushing and shoving following Elijah's death developed did many of them realize they had gone with the wrong side of the doctrinal split.

Ironically, I never was fully inducted into the Muslim movement nor did I participate in the mosque services when released from prison. I went almost directly into the Black Panther political machinery and found there the satisfactions and fulfillments that would last another five tumultuous years. Another split would finally shatter that Panther loyalty and cause me to doubt completely the efficacy of social, political movements as the agent of true liberation or lasting salvation. Everything that I had trusted, supported, and believed had a propensity for melting under the heat and light of testing. At last Jesus would be the One who not only stood and tested time, governments, kingdoms, and nationalities; but I learned with increasing joy that He who was my judge was also my personal Savior. That was to become a sublime discovery and life-changing commitment.

In my Christian life these last two or three years I have had contact with more Black Muslims than Black Panthers. The Panther movement was never as large as the other group, never had the organization and mass appeal that Elijah promoted. His enterprise included businesses, stores, buildings, and major property holdings around the country. He yearned for a Southern state, sort of a pay-off from "white Babylon." Many of these investments, which originally appeared to be big money-makers, turned sour,

even collapsed through poor management and mysterious
money handling by Elijah's top people. I see that his son,
Wallace, has now taken over and talks a most moderate
line in theology and social concern. But it is too late to
really sell the Muslim theology in America—black or white.

I keep running into disillusioned Black Muslims on both
coasts and especially in the Bay Area. Because of the upheaval and doctrinal changes, many of them cannot make
the transition emotionally. It is psychological chaos. Their
problem, which borders on brainwashing, is that they cannot accept a white Jesus. Elijah harped on that miscon-
ception day and night: white Jesus, white cross, white
Christianity. The distortion, stuck in so many Negro minds,
requires patience plus a true understanding of Jesus
Christ, the Semitic peoples, and the worldwide fellowship
of Christians which touches every race, color, and nation-
ality. I find that not only comforting but inspiring.*

Part of my ministry for Christ in the Eldridge Cleaver
Crusades is to meet regularly with these bewildered Muslims. They are desperate and soul-searching and open. I
can see that they want release from the whole Muslim theology which has them so rigidly trapped.

I have wanted to extend my ministry to the Muslims who
are still in prison; and, of course, they number in the
thousands. Of the dozens outside who have come to counsel

---

* In the aftermath of Master Elijah Muhammad's death, a bitter
battle for succession has unfolded between the traditionalist Old
Believers and reformed exponents of a new theology as set forth by
the Honorable Wallace D. Muhammad, son of Elijah. Traditional
dissent from the new theology has rallied around the fiery minister
of New York's Mosque No. 7, Louis Farrakan. Farrakan upholds the
message of Elijah Muhammad, which is a very powerful weapon in
his struggle for supremacy inside the divided and confused ranks
of the nation/world community of Islam.
On February 25, 1978, I attended a mass rally at the Los Angeles
Convention Center, called by the supporters of the Honorable Wallace D. Muhammad. After listening to him explain his new theology,
I am convinced that he has completely outmaneuvered his rivals
and has made a major breakthrough and advance in healing the the-

with me, I have not yet discovered one without a prison record. Seems like everybody from the ghetto has a conviction of a felony: drugs, car theft, draft evasion, smashing glass—something.

Historically, there has been a special game automatically played on the people in the ghetto. Some cops testify today that one of their silent programs was to get a file on every black guy. So, many times they would arrest people totally without cause, just to get the faces and prints on file. They would charge you with something, knowing that you would easily beat it; all was planned so they could have an investigation, then nail your picture and file away your fingerprints. It is disgusting. And that strategy does come back to haunt you, for it seems so easy to jail you later on.

This attitude was confirmed by a friend of mine who works with California's new computerized information network. His job was to program the police computers. Often, he said, he would just sit there and feed names into this giant computer. Individuals who had nothing to do with a conviction or sentence—just pumping in individual names. . . . That has been going on for so many years that by now they must have everyone, including Spiro Agnew and John Mitchell. Cleaver falls between the two . . .

---

ological and spiritual divisions plaguing black Americans. "Remove all racial images from religion" is the major slogan of the movement of Wallace D. Muhammad. This slogan cuts the ground from beneath the feet of people like Farrakan. The slogan also refreshes and renews the challenge which the Black Muslims originally laid at the door of Christianity. The difference now is that Wallace D. Muhammad is challenging both white racism and black racism. Both white theology and black theology stand indicted, and this will become increasingly relevant in the years ahead.

I believe the door is now open for the members of the nation/world community of Islam to be brought to the cross of Jesus Christ. The new teachings of the Honorable Wallace D. Muhammad which sweep away the racist demonology of his father, are a masterpiece of theological metamorphosis. Christians should take every opportunity to reach out to these brothers and sisters.

WHEN I STEPPED OUT of Soledad State Prison into San Francisco in 1966 I sat my feet down in the center of the Haight/Ashbury. I embraced it, wallowed in it. For years, in prison, I had watched this scene develop, watched it grow deeper, and had come to certain conclusions about it. I saw in this ferment, this turning away in alienation and rebellion, this total disgust with the old and avid hunger for a new life, a new reality—I saw in this the readiness of a quorum of the people to shatter the existing structure of oppression and repression that I had come to call, with loathing, Babylon.

You met people in the Haight who had started out walking six months ago, fleeing from the smothering fog of a country lost and wandering blindly through the swamps of its own hypocrisy and rotten with the corruption of its every value. People trekked to the Haight to escape the cacophony of Babylon, the clank and clatter of a trussed up butcher shop of a society busy slaughtering the innocence and conscience of its youth in sleek, swift sacrifice to the dead gods of avarice and power. They poured into the Haight to escape, and, most important, to find a new life. The Haight was at the end of the rainbow of the broken spectrum of the American mind. If you made it to the Haight, you would be saved, born again, delivered from the doom that was enveloping the land.

There was a poison wind blowing throughout the wilderness of Babylon, pouring up out of the manholes of Wall Street, Madison Avenue, the Pentagon, the White House, the Congress, the Supreme Court, the churches, universi-

80

ties, colleges, and even the campuses of high schools, and out of every home—a noxious poison oozing out of every porous institution of American life. The elders, consumed by this poison, contaminated beyond retrieval by the power of any antidote, were doomed, and lacked even the dimmest potentiality of comprehending either the catastrophe of their dead-end lives, or the frenzied efforts of their own children to ward off a heritage that threatened to anchor them down in the pit. Lyndon Johnson was trying to bomb the Vietnamese back into the Stone Age, but he had succeeded only in blowing the American mind out of its own sockets. The counterrevolution that had begun with the assassination of President Kennedy was in full swing to the right, and the torch that had been lighted by ten years of struggle had been brutally extinguished on the threshold of a new frontier.

A darkness now prevailed in Babylon, a civilization had been plunged into its deepest, darkest night, and it was sinking farther every minute under the thrust of its own dead weight. There was not a politician in sight who could save us, and the hatchet man cum statesman lurked behind every ballot box and haunted the halls of every official building on the continent. So we sought refuge in the streets. The Haight became the symbol of that quest in its manifestation among the white people, for, above all, what was happening in the Haight was a white scene.

It was an explosion that had been building up for a long time, for at least ten years, building toward this head, powered by drugs, sex, and a raging wrath against the form and content of the social order. What had once been an amorphous, disoriented, and innocuous ferment of discontent, spreading like an epidemic among a genre of whites, had written its own history and taken on definite shape. It had been influenced and delimited by the thrust of the struggle going on among black people, defined at

the edges where it touched the black thing. The primary
contact had been black music: jazz, rhythm and blues, and
that step child, rock and roll. But the clincher had been
the nonviolent civil rights movement, which attracted
whites by the droves, organized their politics, and alien-
ated them from the established power structure.

During the latter half of the 1950s, the Cuban Revolution
—Fidel, Che, long hair and beards, the Sierra Maestra
Mountains, Havana—became a focus of American dissent.
Oriented on the ABCs of the domestic scene by the civil
rights movement of blacks, American dissenters were glued
in on the ABCs of the international situation from the experience and perspective of supporting and defending Fidel
Castro and the Cuban Revolution. By the time LBJ started
heavy bombing in Vietnam, white America was in the middle of a freak-out—freaked out because their relationship
to power, to the government, to the Constitution, and to
everything else holy in the cosmos of the American mind
was naked, and the proportions of the nightmare were
clearly revealed.

Drugs, as a surrogate for violent revolution, became the
vehicle of a nationwide Boston Tea Party, of the turning
away of a people from a government divorced from the
consent of the governed, as sex stretched to new proportions and lay down in a groove to new music. Stoned,
angry to the point of rebellion, and fornicating themselves
into a new relationship to their bodies, these dissenters
were searching for meaning in their lives. What they pro-
duced was a new religion. They were burning their brains
out with acid, scorching their nerves with speed, and in
the words of Timothy Leary, they were turning on, tuning
in, and dropping out. Having survived the ravages of the
'50s and the withering torch of the first half of the '60s,
Allen Ginsberg, tinkling his fairy bells, had lived to see the
triumph of the sentiment reflected in the poem "Howl,"

which got him over a decade earlier. The Moloch of his terror, the agony of his "Howl," was still there, hoary, still dripping blood; Allen Ginsberg's triumph was that hordes of just white tribal brothers and sisters were now howling with him.

Long before I got out of prison, I had made a conscious decision to do my thing, to go all the way out on the limb, because that's where the flowers have gone. The flower I wanted was the red rose of a real revolution, a revolution that would kill all those members of the ruling class who refused to abdicate and surrender, those who continued to resist, and especially those who were actively opposed. That's how I felt about it. Shaping the thing into ordinary rhetoric: I wanted a social, political, and economic revolution along socialist lines. I wanted an end to the capitalist economic system, and for the natural resources, technology, and all information to be taken out of the control of the individuals, families, groups, and corporate entities that owned them as private property. I wanted them to be recognized as belonging to all the people. Most of all, I hated prisons. There was nothing in life that I hated more than a prison, recognizing prison to be no more and no less than the ultimate degree of restraint, this side of the final restraint of execution, legally or illegally imposed.

So I hated all social controls as they existed. I hated the state, especially the mechanism of the State of California, which I knew in detail, but all the other states, separately and combined, too. I hated jobs, courts, departments, agencies, sections, divisions, jails, branches, boards, committees, institutions, corporations, foundations, Chambers of Commerce, associations, unions—they were all like cells of the same cancerous tissue, along with cell block, unit, isolation, adjustment center, death row.

It was a sickening brew of all these jobs and titles, these digital calibrations of the contours of a monstrous system, in which we existed—walking, stumbling as though in a dream, seemingly through a maze, which nobody seemed to understand, caught up in a social entity, situation, and process that was as abstract and formless as the spiral in the tail of a galaxy spinning through a universe of space. And, over the years, I had refined my own technique of jazzing with the man, keeping him uptight. I had survived, doing my thing, the prison system of the State of California.

The linking up with Bobby Seale and Huey Newton following my release from prison was a natural and exciting transition. Increasingly, it appeared that the main interest of the Muslim movement was to create ghetto businesses and sell bean pies. Later, the murder of Martin Luther King, Jr., following the death of Elijah Muhammad and the killing of Malcolm X, *would propel the black community beyond the dictates of nonviolence, and certainly beyond the mentality of creating a future out of 5- and 10-cent stores in the ghetto. It was the moment of challenge and change. The challenge must be shoved right into the face of the racist leaders, the oppressive establishment of America. The change had to come within the hearts and minds of Negroes all over North America.*

5

PANTHERS AND POWER

IN THE FALL OF 1967 the time and conditions were ripe for the sudden rise of the Black Panthers. The other major civil rights group that had high visibility and a cutting edge on the question of Vietnam and racism was the Student Non-violent Coordination Committee. SNCC had some very articulate leaders in Stokely Carmichael, Rap Brown, and James Forman. They shared with King a hope that meaningful and lasting change would come without revolutionary bloodshed. Yet their militancy was sharp and eager. Their point of reference was not the ghetto but the college campuses of America, starting within the black colleges. After making initial contact with SNCC as an observer of their campus program for *Ramparts* magazine, I joined Stokely on his speaking tour of the college circuit, got acquainted with many of their national staff, and saw the potential for expanded leadership that lay within the organization.

But first, Kathleen Neal. . . .

The greatest urgency that propelled me in those post-prison months of 1967–68 was to get married. I wanted to get married tomorrow. I knew that I would marry a black woman, and I am not the least surprised that I fell in love with Kathleen. I first met her at SNCC headquarters in Nashville. She and other SNCC women there were the perfect image of Negro militancy. Beautiful, smart, well-groomed, put together with a driving intensity, they had become legendary—especially those out of Mississippi.

All over America young Negroes talked about the SNCC women, and I suppose I too was caught up in the fantasy and myth that surrounded their work and example. I remember saying to friends on the Coast, "I've got to get me one of those SNCC gals for a wife. They have the future inside. I've just got to marry one of those gals."

One day I went into the headquarters house in Nashville where all the SNCC people had assembled. There was this girl typing, and it was Kathleen. I started after her right there! I had never believed in love at first sight; it was impossible and ridiculous. But it happened to me. When I first saw her, she was sitting there typing at an incredible speed. Zooooooooooooom went the keys of her electric machine. I was absolutely married at that office introduction.

It was a perfect match. She was highly educated, a college person, liked books and was always ready to talk about the issues. She also had a lot of raw nerve; the Klan and the White Citizens Council never fazed her. Neither would the later police break-ins in the middle of the night nor the confrontation with the Algerian army. It was a perfect match on all levels, and I have considered it one of the two best decisions of my life.

Once, when I would meet a girl that I thought I wanted to marry, I would take her by my mother's house in Los Angeles, and Mother would say, "Phew." I took several by and always Mother would make this put-down sound with her lips. But when she met Kathleen, she didn't make a sound, just smiled and hugged her. It seems that the whole world wants to hug Kathleen.

The merger of the SNCC organization into the Black Panthers was a natural but not easy hookup. Racial conflagrations in the American cities had shut down the future of the nonviolent speech makers. The death of King in the spring of 1968 shook Stokely and Rap and James Forman right down to their sneakers. They had grown up within the safety and protection of the black middle class, the black bourgeoisie—and while they could use some daring language and point to threatening events, it all was played out on the secure carpet of a college dormitory, a student union ballroom or campus parking lot.

So when the gunfire started and the plastic bombs were going off smartly, and people like Martin King getting shot down in Southern motels, a real chill went through the SNCC leadership. It was clear to me that the internal structure of their movement was wavering. They had a big following of volunteers, especially young people and particularly, dedicated coeds. The Panthers needed a broad national following. We were too anchored to several urban ghettoes, and that was it.

When the merger really got on wheels, Stokely Carmichael and his faction was hot for it, but Rap Brown and James Forman held back. You needed titles for everyone. I thought Stokely could be Prime Minister of the Black Nation and Rap Brown could be the Comedian, sort of a black Will Rogers. He was full of clever remarks.

The severity of the times made the merger necessary,

and the presence of the Black Panthers made it possible. For we were not the Bible belt but the gun belt. The SNCCs had come out of the Southern rural tradition; we were off the ghetto pavement and rather prepared for the sound of gunfire. When Stokely and Rap and some others first appeared at the Los Angeles airport following the final merger, I had a delegation meet them, like body-guards and a big show of rifles and shotguns. They gulped as much as the airport security personnel. Funny, how the arrangement of social mores in America made it O.K. for a white to walk around with a gun, have one hanging across the back window of his pickup, or go out shooting on Saturday afternoon; but let three or four Negroes walk downtown or out to the airport with a few firearms, and the lights would come on and the sirens wail.

Well, we gave them plenty to think about. The only way to deal with violence which was shedding its grace all over the United States—and rather thoroughly in Vietnam —was to pack some ourselves. I was very much at home with this, and my swift rise in the Panther leadership circle came from two sources: my celebrity status as the best-selling author of *Soul on Ice* and my ghetto back-ground which never choked at the sight or sound of a gun.

The Black Panther movement was never a mass activity. We were a vanguard organization with rigid entry stand-ards, rules, and regulations. Even with the influx of SNCC people, the courtship of the communists, and the fan letters of the Weathermen, we had more followers than actual members. When the crisis came down in 1968, our ranks really thinned out. There were many white sympa-thizers, and the anti-Vietnam War coalition swelled the ranks when a public rally was required. But our style and strategy did not lend itself to developing a big, mass mem-bership.

For one thing, we were into such heavy, dangerous confrontation that nothing could be accomplished with a cast of thousands. Our leadership of Huey, Bobby, and myself was under constant surveillance and harrassment by the police. It seemed that one of us was always in jail or waiting trial or out on bond. Our energy and resources were regularly stretched to the limit. Without the arrival of SNCC and the generous money support of many liberals, we could not have operated as long as we did.

Much of the money that kept us going—and gave me travel funds for the final flight to Cuba—was the sale of my book. *Soul on Ice* also brought to the Panther organization a certain articulate status that lifted us above the normal rhetoric of the street and cell. Some brothers were very good with one-liners but were not much after dumping a few slogans. For a while I was caught up in revolutionary rhetoric and said "off the pig" and "right on" at every intersection. The pig nomenclature came out of Huey Newton's rage toward the usurpation of police powers.

I remember the day that we were pulling together an editorial for our Panther newspaper. It was my task to gather up the material, get the grammar right, and see that the misprints were kept under control. Huey was dictating a polemic against the police for a recent unjust arrest they had committed. He had had a confrontation with this big cop and he was calling him every name imaginable: swine, fat belly, and pig—"That's it," he said. "That's what he was—a pig!" From that time forward, we used the word. I found a picture of a pig from a postcard, cut it out, and put that policeman's badge number on the pig.

Terminology

The employment of the term "pig" was already endorsed by the Muslim theology. Its circulation in the Negro community had wide acceptance. Elijah Muhammad would often say that a pig was one-third cat, one-third dog, and one-third rat. He taught the orthodox position concerning pork, and this did create problems within the ghetto, for pork was a lot cheaper than beef steak. Many brothers had a light meal in prison when pork sausage or pork chops were served.

The Black Panthers absorbed much of the Black Muslim vocabulary, particularly the idea of the Beast—which Elijah Muhammad identified from the Book of Revelation as Babylon America. These names were used to describe the cruelty and animality of white devil America. They became essential to my own word list; and when Lee Lockwood interviewed me in Algiers, there was one sequence which illustrates my point:

Lockwood: Why did you say "Babylon"?

Cleaver: Because of all the symbols that I've ever run across to indicate a decadent society, I find the term Babylon, which I take from Revelation in the Bible, to be the most touching. That's how they describe Babylon—as a decadent society. . . .

Lockwood: It's an analogue?

Cleaver: It's an analogue. The United States of America is described in Revelation. I'm not being a prophet. I'm just saying that I dig that.*

Panther Possibilities

The philosophical thrust of the Panther movement can be seen in the use of the term "pig." And that should be seen in contrast to the Black Muslim doctrine which built so much hatred on the white community in America—

* Lee Lockwood, *Conversation with Eldridge Cleaver* (New York: McGraw-Hill, 1970) p. 53.

something that I did not share personally and felt to be debilitating for black progress. It would often irritate my black companions that I never developed the vehemence they expressed toward whitey. My attitude was shaped by my mother who always insisted that there were good and bad whites and good and bad negroes, etc. She never backed up on that teaching and never permitted her children to blame the problems of the world on the white people—just some of them.

Naturally I modified that impression, but I also alternated some of the Black Muslim thought that was seeping into Panther rhetoric. To me it seemed intolerable that the black community should be taught to hate the white devils as proscribed by Elijah Muhammad. That was adding a reverse amount of racism to an already complex system, so I pushed our teachings in another direction.

From my friend John Hall and the Marxist writings that he gave me, I learned the Communist method of social analysis. I was quite enamored with Karl Marx and the *Communist Manifesto*. In prison I spent many hours working through the heavy writings of Marx and Engels. I borrowed from them their logic and understanding of social-political and economic systems. I gained the capacity to interpret what was happening in America and saw a ruling clique in charge. Therefore, it seemed imperative to concentrate on the true oppressors—those who were enslaving whites as well as blacks—and not make wild generalizations, à là Muslims, that we had to hate the white devil, do our own thing, and everything would work out.

Panther Program

As I have remarked earlier, the King assassination accelerated the conflicts and confrontations during 1968. Before that April shoot-out in Oakland, Panthers had been

eager to arm the ghetto, to insure the personal protection
of black people, and to instruct members in the use of
sophisticated weapons. We issued manuals for the use of
semiautomatic arms; we had our own shooting galleries;
office closets were crammed with ready to use firearms.
The show-and-tell of carrying armor was very important.
In fact, the very first impression that I had of the Black
Panther movement, and the first time that I met Newton
and Seale and two other brothers, was at a meeting to
plan a memorial service for Malcolm X. A gathering of
black organizations had assembled to decide who would
say what. When the Panthers arrived, I later wrote in
Ramparts:

> I spun around in my seat and saw the most beautiful sight I
> had ever seen: four black men wearing black berets, powder
> blue shirts, black leather jackets, black trousers, shiny black
> shoes—and each with a gun. In front was Huey P. Newton
> with a riot pump shotgun in his right hand, barrel pointed
> down to the floor. Beside him was Bobby Seale, the handle
> of a .45 caliber automatic showing from its holster on his
> right hip . . . who are these cats? I wondered at them,
> checking them out carefully.*

As Minister of Information, I carefully prepared the
writings and speeches of Newton and Seale for public
consumption. We had our own newspaper going, and the
imprisonment of Newton only intensified the need for
public relations and public information. My own incarcera-
tion from April to June of 1968 did not slow down my
efforts, since material was smuggled out of Vacaville and
pushed into the ever-hungry media. The top three leaders
of the Panther Party were in great demand by civil rights
groups, anti-war groups, militant student organizations,

---

* Letter of June 15, 1968, describing a meeting in February 1967
for *Ramparts.*

and a host of ghetto activist units. While I always considered myself a better writer than speaker, the events kept pressing me to make public pronouncements and, more frequently, major addresses.

The first big breakthrough for me, publicly, came a year earlier at the massive anti-war rally in Kezar Stadium in San Francisco. Some 65,000 yelling, chanting, fist-clenching war protesters showed up to hear Mrs. Martin Luther King. I also spoke and gained not only the attention of the peace movement but also the wrath of my parole officers. A couple of days later, two of them let me *know* that I would be back in the lockup if I made any more speeches *like that*. Here I was out on parole—out from serving the complete term for assault and now being threatened a return penalty for being a political activist. The insidious oppression of the white power structure really hit home. My determination to be freely vocal rose with every new threat from the Adult Correction Authority, which managed all people on parole and probation in California.

Panther popularity would reach a zenith in the latter months of 1968. The trial of Huey Newton was bringing the press to a boil, and the celebrity attention I was getting in places like the *New York Times* also afforded me a certain amount of protection and security. The cops could no longer just wash me away on some sidewalk. Now they had to have large reasons to match their large hatred for this mass meeting monster.

During this period it was evident to me that black consciousness and black nation awareness was one way that the Negro community could start to focus on their powerlessness and begin to appreciate more fully the Black Panther program. I suggested that the United Nations be called to supervise a plebiscite within the black communities of America, the purpose being to find out what the

Negroes of our country really wanted. Did the black masses consider themselves a nation, for instance? Would they like to have membership in the United Nations? (Not so far-fetched for thirty million people. Today several of the Indian nations of North America are asking the same question.)

Among Panther theorists like myself, it seemed an ideal measure to put Uncle Sam on the spot, for the Washington policy response would surely be the argument that Americans did not need U.N. membership since they were U.S. citizens. And the instant black remark, especially the millions in the ghetto, would be, "Well, if I'm an American citizen, why am I treated like a dog?" We especially wanted to raise the discussion to the international level—after Brother Malcolm—with all the spotlights glowing.

All of this writing prepared my readers for what followed—a rationale for urban guerrilla warfare. I suggested that the liberation for Afro-Americans from the white colonial bondage in this country, should be spearheaded at the point of the gun. I was specific: "Black urban guerrillas now dream of liberating black communities with the gun by eliminating America's police power over black people, i.e., by breaking the power of the mother country over the black colony."

More and more our editorials and pronouncements urged the possession and training of black people with weapons of defense. We taught that a well-armed ghetto would at least be not so vulnerable to capricious police raids and the routine destruction of personal and civil rights guaranteed by the Constitution. We were definitely against gun control as well as mind control. I concluded one article by saying:

Black men know they must pick up the gun, they must arm black people to the teeth, they must organize an army and confront the mother country with a most drastic consequence if she attempts to assert police power over the colony. If the white mother country is to have victory over the black colony, it is the duty of black revolutionaries to insure that the Imperialists receive no more than a Pyrrhic victory, written in the blood of what America might have become.*

It was altogether appropriate that we picked as the slogan for the Black Panther Party a quote from Chairman Mao in the Little Red Book. "We are the advocates of the abolition of war; we do not want war; but war can only be abolished through war; and in order to get rid of the gun, it is necessary to pick up the gun."

Our feelings, commitment, and enthusiasm were total for revolution. The attempts and slander of police powers to paint us as urban gangsters never made sense—except to them. For if they had to deal with us as political personalities, with a distinct vision and plan to implement that cause, another stance was required. For some who were opposed to our existence, the frequent references to Chinese Communist doctrine and my own personal fascination with Joseph Stalin (picture on the office wall), may have added fuel to their lethal fire. J. Edgar Hoover certainly believed that he had every reason to put us underground, forever. The visibility of weapons, the anti-war protests, the Marxist slogans, and the editorials that I pushed out helped to make his nights uneasy.

I had lived defiantly so long and in such seething hatred of all governments, people in power, people in charge, that when I came under the shelter of Communist powers, I sadly discovered that their corruption was as violent and inhuman as the people they "victoriously" replaced. "Up against the wall" was a trendy slogan of the underground movements around the world—but I later learned that without inner control, a moral perspective, and a spiritual

---

* *Ramparts*, April-May 1968.

balance that flowed out of Christian love, justice, and caring, the Communist promises were to become the largest fraud of all.

Pig power in America was infuriating—but pig power in the Communist framework was awesome and unaccountable. No protection by outbursts in the press and electronic media—the Reds owned it. No shelter under the benevolent protection of a historic constitution—the Marxists held the book and they tore out the pages that sheltered you. No counterweight from religious and church organizations—they were invisible and silent.

My adult education began in prison and was ruefully completed in the prison that is called Marxist liberation, "power to the people": that was meant for the party in control, writing the script, and enforcing the rules. I did mean it deeply when I said seven years later that I would rather be in prison in America than free somewhere else.

IF YOU THINK WE were hectic in our planning and frantic in our operations, consider the busy life of J. Edgar Hoover and his thousands of agents. They were positive that we were the enemy, and they tracked us hourly. Our meetings were covered by monitoring devices and double agents. Our telephone conversations, our mail, and our every outside movement seemed to be shadowed by someone from the other side. In the summer months of 1968, following the Oakland event and the outcry for Huey's release (we were certain that he was going to the gas chamber with whatever the evidence that the State could muster or manufacture), my day/night hours were hardly private. I remember a period during which I never went to the same place at night, changed my travel routes around the San Francisco Bay area on the spur of the moment, running entirely on impulse and random selection of streets and freeways. I ended up one evening at a friend's house, and I wasn't there twenty minutes when the telephone rang. We looked at each other—this was a private, confidential meeting, we thought. The voice on the other end said, "Hi, Eldridge, just didn't want you to think that we had forgotten you." Click. I was never forgotten.

For years we were the best thing that ever came along for Mr. Hoover at budget time before Congress. In December of 1970 J. Edgar told the Byrd Committee that his bureau would need at least $14.1 million in additional funds to hire 1,000 extra FBI agents plus 702 clerks to back them up. He noted that 600 would be assigned to the organized crime prevention division and the other 400 to survey radical activities, including airline hijacking. By now, we had become his bread and butter; and when I left America, he hobbied on the Berrigan brothers, claiming that they had planned to kidnap a high government official and disrupt federal government operations in the District of Columbia.

Hoover was half-right. We were starting to devise ways of throwing the white establishment into chaos, but this was much more serious than he allowed in his report to the Senate Appropriations Committee.

The injustices of the power structure in America toward the black community and the outrageous war in Southeast Asia were providing a double-barreled onslaught to the people in charge. I was asked to run for President on the ticket of the Peace and Freedom Party—a strategy to reveal the strength and agitation that was now reaching into so many white and black homes. More than 100,000 people in California signed petitions for the party to be on the November ballot. About this time, I noted that there was a "little bit of George Wallace in every white American." I also was invited to give lectures at the University of California at Berkeley. This turned the state school system upside down. Governor Reagan issued all sorts of warnings, and Max Rafferty, directly in charge of public instruction, threatened education's demise. They both launched into my classroom appearances with the inspiration of holy war. The effect was marvelous. There was enormous support from young people all over the West, particularly on the large college campuses.

My own feeling of paranoia was rocketing during this fall season of 1968. I was out again on parole, thanks to the ruling of Judge Sherwin. But his writ of habeas corpus was soon overruled by the California Appeals Court, and they ordered me to surrender to prison officials on November 27, 1968. The atmosphere was charged not only with the tension of the presidential elections, but also the clamoring within the Panther organization that we really had to free Huey Newton or go down trying. Many of the brothers were so tight that they wanted a major shoot-out with the police establishment, and, unfortunately, this was supported momentarily by Newton. He was under heavy guard at San Quentin. It was only with the greatest difficulty that anyone could see him. Security was presidential, and his own paranoia was functioning at a fever pitch. He kept telling people, in person and by message, that he wanted a "red light finale."

The "red light finale" was the ultimate fulfillment for a revolutionary's death wish. What Newton was saying: "Don't let them toy with me and then march me down to some stinking gas chamber. Life should be more vivid, more gutsy than that. I wanted a red light finale, with the police cars screaming through the night, lights flashing, and hours of gunfire, with the Panther forces attacking and breaking into San Quentin." Well, it sounded very romantic to the younger, gun-toting Panthers. To this aged convict, it was ridiculous. These office people were too distant from reality. None of them had been in the Big Place. You don't just walk up to a guard, stick a shotgun in his face and say, "Give me the keys." They had no idea that it was thirteen stories, with elevators, plus machine gun placements, plus a lot of other secret devices that even the Warden has forgotten.

I finally got to Huey and told him to forget that motion picture scenario. There was no way that a mass assault would work. He would be shot instantly inside, and a lot of dead Panthers would be stretched out on the parkways of California, barely making it to the gates of the prison. Reason prevailed, or at least deterred, the wilder gun-slingers. . . .

The Party was desperate to get some leverage on the

white power structure that had us more and more on the defensive. Some of the leadership wanted a private plane assault on all the prisons of California, with our people landing within the walls and freeing everyone inside. Thousands of Panther-oriented prisoners would be released, and our grand strategy for guerrilla warfare against Washington could commence. Others wanted to kidnap the black athletes at the Mexico City Olympics. Revolutionaries from Mexico had come up to talk with me and urged a commando attack against the Games, with the kidnapping of prominent stars.

By now a steady flow of military equipment and pilfered supplies was showing up in our armory. Military depots and national guard armories leaked like sieves. Some armaments were sold to us; others were gifts for the Movement. It was happening all over America, and the government was aware that our gear was in a state of readiness. Long-range strategy favored a scattering of guerrilla forces—actually small, self-contained cells of a dozen or less—in the great metropolitan areas of the United States, with significant clusters hidden in the mountains of America. Our conviction was that the government would become more oppressive and more intolerable. The Vietnam war was sinking in its own decay. Popular support had vanished, for even white grandmothers were marching against the military. It was my contention that whites would outnumber blacks in their revulsion for the war insanity and eventually turn against the powers that sustained it. At that point, a massive, bloodletting upheaval would take place, and the blacks as well as enraged whites would seize ultimate power.

It is my belief today that the court sentencing of John Mitchell, Bob Haldeman, and John Ehrlichmann did more to restore the affection and support of blacks for their government than anything else in the last twenty-five years.

Everyone in the ghetto was saying, "Well, Mitchell won't go to jail. Rockefeller will get him off; the fix is in." But Big John is in the cooler, the Constitution proved stronger than the cries of San Clemente, and the whole lying crowd was thrown out of office. Must have made Moscow shudder and Castro cough. There are times when America is just plain beautiful.

Every movement has its idealism, and I had bought the Marxist line rather fully when reading it in prison. The pay-off in human affairs seemed so contrary, even opposite, to what I had come to expect, however. I was used to America defaulting on its democratic principles, but the Marxists never demonstrated anything better to me in the countries I visited. As a guest, I carefully promoted their party line back to the United States and into various Panther publications, but inwardly my doubts and dismay were growing.

6

COMMUNISM: ITS
FLOWERS AND THORNS

THE LOCATING OF A Black Panther training facility in Cuba
had been proposed by Castro's people in New York—in
fact, by their representative to the United Nations. There
was much excitement over the possibilities of a building
or units, surrounded by acres of revolutionary camps and
personnel, all working rigorously for the glorious invasion
of America. I do not mean to be sarcastic now; but in
retrospect, the grand design seems pretty ridiculous and
unreal. Our highest hope was to have a center in the Caribbean that would prepare revolutionary cadres to slink
back into the United States, many to blend with the urban
scene and function as guerrillas on that sidewalk level.
No major confrontations with the army and police, no

battle at Little Big Horn or Gettysburg, but much disruption and chipping away at a decaying power structure that was becoming increasingly anti-democratic and invariably more fascist.

The other trained and equipped forces would be dropped into the mountain area of North America. The plan here was to have small mobile units that could shift easily in and out of rural areas, living off the land, and tying up thousands of troops in fruitless pursuit. What turned out to be fruitless was the reality of such a camp in Cuba. I sat in my apartment wondering if I was the enemy in the eyes of nervous Cuban security guards.

In 1969 I had sent a cassette recording back to friends in the United States warning how insidious and dangerous was the white racism of the Castro dictatorship in Cuba. That warning had been a distillation of views expressed to me by Captain Toro, a young black Cuban army officer home on leave from fighting against the Portuguese in Guinea-Bissau.

Toro, as I reported in the May 3, 1976, issue of *Newsweek*, had bitterly denounced Castro's policy of shipping militant young black officers out to foreign wars, a maneuver that implied his support of the fight for black people's rights while actually designed for getting rid of troublemakers at home. Castro, according to Toro, had come to power because he was "the last white hope of the traditional Cuban ruling class, which, given the choice between a black-led revolution and a white one, had chosen Fidel." Unsuccessful in his attempt to disarm the Cuban blacks, he had found it "safe" to ship them off to Africa.

His motives became apparent in the collapse of a guerrilla movement in the Congo following the death of Patrice Lumumba in 1961. Che Guevara had been sent to aid Mulele's guerrilla forces, but on the eve of achieving his objective, was recalled by a specially coded secret message from Castro. Ange Diawara, the political commissar of the army of the Congo, later told me that "everybody understood that Castro was pulling Che out of the Congo because of pressure from the Soviets, who had arranged things with the Americans. This was the fundamental betrayal of the African revolution."

While in overseas exile, I discovered the frequency with which I was lecturing the hard-rock mentality of Communist leaders, reminding them that the world revolution was deeply rooted in the American people. I had heard so much rhetoric in every Communist country about their glorious leaders and their incredible revolutionary spirit that even to this very angry and disgruntled American, it was absurd and unreal. To their irritation and dismay, I continually pointed out that the United States of America had glorified the word "revolution," that we had profoundly contributed to the spirit of political liberty for all people everywhere. It never failed to rouse resentment when I got on this theme, but there was no way it could or should be avoided.

Communists like to play at history. The line between fact and fiction, on the surface, was often blurred, or at least the spiel they mouthed was purposely vague at important historic intersections. I noted over and over again, in Algeria, Central Africa, North Korea, China, and North Vietnam that the American people had a very deep respect for the individual and his rights. Consequently, I was angry and upset that my own country had violated those rights by the war in Vietnam and the oppression of the blacks and other minorities at home. But in the same breath, in what must have seemed like nigger arrogance to the bright Communist translators and their glaring Communist leaders, I noted that their own countries never enjoyed this tradition; it was not in their social and political bloodstream.

Convincing illustrations of my argument jumped out with frightening regularity: here was Russia coming from the tradition of Czarist rule—rigid and lethal monarchies. Here was China with its dynasties of emperors for thousands of years; here was Cuba, which most recently had traded a tyrannical sergeant for a Communist dictator. These people of Marxist persuasion and communist doctrine could never answer my deliverance on human rights in America. What answer could they give?

The longer I stayed in these foreign enclaves, the more I realized that America could not be instructed, by them, in anything that had to do with individual rights or personal liberty. The inner recesses of my being, the secret soul of my most honest self was developing a searing resentment against the ridiculous claims of communism. If they couldn't convince me, I thought, how are they going to ever sell the rest of the world and keep them sold! I decided they were not.

That really, was the official end of my emotional exile from the United States. While it would take some years to return, the fugitive heart, the prodigal spirit had already come home.

THE PANTHER PARTY was comfortable in the Sixties with certain public pronouncements of the Communists in America. Our ten-point Panther program had centered on the self-determination and self-development of the black community. Marxists in America were hot for this goal and offered to give us assistance in reaching it. Unfortunately, that cooperation never reached a relevant point, and I began to sense that the Reds were opportunists for their own enhancement rather than activists in search of social justice for blacks.

While I personally was turned on to the ruthless power of Joseph Stalin, the quotations of Chairman Mao were catchy and his Little Red Book available at different outlets in California. By 1969 *The Black Panther* paper was saturated with Mao slogans. Huey once wrote, "Brother Mao put that quite well. We will follow the pattern and follow the thoughts of Chairman Mao." (He was referring to the Chinese leader's classic comment: "In the near future a colossal event will occur where the masses of people will rise up like a mighty storm and a hurricane, sweeping all evil gentry and corrupt officials into their graves.")

The Panthers were living on the borderline between life and death, success and failure; so words from older, established revolutionaries had a special ring for our desperate moment. We believed the Little Red Book when it said, "Where there is struggle, there is sacrifice, and death is a common occurrence."

As the thoughts and philosophy of Chairman Mao became more popular within the party rhetoric, so did his style of operation and discipline. The Panthers were never a tightly run, cohesive national body. Metropolitan groups would spring up, using our name and showing pictures of Huey and Bobby and me, but their operations were often vague and their motivations puzzling. Some of them masqueraded as Panthers and pursued gangster goals. Others were on drugs, selling and taking, and that was forbidden. Discipline was constantly a hassle and enforcement a real challenge for the people running the party. Factions and splits were a constant threat to the viability of the organization. When twenty-one Panthers were read out of the party in a 1969 purge, the Omaha, Nebraska, branch issued this statement, straight out of the Little Red Book:

We must affirm anew the discipline of the Party, namely:
1. Individual is subordinate to the organization
2. The minority is subordinate to the majority
3. The lower level is subordinate to the higher level
4. The entire membership is subordinate to the Central Committee.

Whoever violates these articles of discipline disrupts Party unity.

In August of 1969 Willie McIntyre was expelled from the Philadelphia branch of the party. When the official expulsion was publicly announced, the following item was taken from Chairman Mao, a sign of correct revolutionary procedure: "Not to obey orders but to give pride of place to one's own opinions. To demand special consideration from the organization but to reject its discipline."

There were some aspects of Chairman Mao's thought and direction that had helpful and sensitive application for the life of the Panthers in the ghetto. This philosophy was to penetrate and correct much of the thoughtless violence that could infect any gathering of professional thugs, drug

runners, rapists, and muggers. We would ask our members
to recite the guidelines Mao taught his revolutionary forces
in China:

1. Speak politely.
2. Pay fairly for what you buy.
3. Return everything you borrow.
4. Pay for anything you damage.
5. Do not hit or swear at people.
6. Do not damage crops.
7. Do not take liberties with women.
8. Do not ill-treat captives.

Those still stand as a model for any army, with or without
a revolution to justify their existence.

While the ten points of the Black Panther party were
filled with demands and righteous expectations, they were
not fashioned from the Little Red Book nor written in
Moscow. Perhaps that is why we could never get Communist money support when we really needed it. We were
pushing our program, not theirs, but willing to borrow
their strategy, and at times, their vocabulary:

1. Freedom. We want power to determine the destiny
   of black communities.
2. Employment. We want full employment for all our
   people.
3. Housing. We demand housing fit for the shelter of
   human beings.
4. Military Service. We want black men exempted from
   military service.
5. Education. We demand decent education for black
   people—an education that teaches the truth about
   this decadent, racist society; and teaches black children their rightful place in society.
6. Business. We want an end to the robbery of black
   people in their own communities by white business
   interests.

7. Police. We demand an end to police brutality and the murder of black people in America.

8. Justice. We want the release of all black men held in city, county, state, and federal jails. Since they have not had fair trials, but received a Nazi-form of justice, like a Jew tried in Nazi-Germany. We demand their release.

9. Fair Juries. We demand the trial of black people before black juries—trial by one's peers who come from the same economic, social, religious, historical, and racial community.

10. Land. We want land, just as we want clothing, housing, education, justice, money and peace.

The Panther program was essentially an attempt to redress the injustices of the black community, suffered for more than two hundred years. Much of the input may be traced to the Black Muslims, some to the Communists, but all of it rang a bell in the minds of deprived ghetto citizens: we wanted control of our lives.

MANY PEOPLE HAVE the idea that, once upon a time, America was a peaceful Garden of Eden and then along came the Black Panther Party which in turn gave rise to chaos. That is a patently false impression, but one that was deliberately fostered both by ignorant opinion and hostile misrepresentation. When the Black Panther Party was founded in October 1966, America had already gone over the deep end. The war was raging, had been raging for years, in Vietnam. The Supreme Court decision in 1954, outlawing the doctrine of separate-but-equal and ushering in a new level of black struggle for freedom and equality, was already twelve years old. Its greatest confrontations, both in the halls of Congress and in the streets of America, were all but forgotten. Martin Luther King, Jr., had already won his Nobel Prize, and the Montgomery bus boycott at its root was long since over. King had addressed the March on Washington, the noblest assembly of the American people of our era, and the president who had made it possible, who had welcomed King to the White House and arrested George Wallace, had been assassinated three years before. In two more years, King himself would be assassinated. The quiet that had fallen over black America when Malcolm X was killed had been shattered. The Watts uprising, first fruit of Malcolm's prophetic call for armed self-defense, signaled the dramatic transformation of the black movement from the philosophical perspective of nonviolence, to meeting violence with violence. President Lyndon Johnson was not far from announcing his retirement and repudiation. All this had already happened. There was chaos in America.

115

That was the brew from which the Black Panther Party sprang, dedicated to bringing some order out of the chaos, because black people were being killed in unprecedented number. City after city was exploding. The National Guard became a fact of life. Richard Nixon ran for president on a platform pledged to bring order to that very same chaos, but from a completely different set of plans and points of view.

In response to those riotous eruptions in Watts, Detroit, New York, New Jersey, and points in between, the authorities saturated black communities throughout America with emergency forces. Police departments doubled and tripled their patrols—a sudden introduction of a standing army into occupied territory. The mere presence of this force increased the statistically predictable conflicts between those who lived in the occupied territory and the foreign troops. The number one demand in the black community became an end to police brutality. Police brutality was at the core of the explosions, because they had been called in to defend the status quo. Black people were refusing to knuckle under, to be corralled and controlled by the police, and the opposing forces were ordering the police to control and contain black people. There was the contradiction and the confrontation. The act of aggression had already taken place, we were already under the heel; so that our response, no matter what it was—another scream of protest, another petition filed before the same old judges, or to hit back, to return the fire—this time, was justified, clearly. On the day of its founding, Huey and Bobby named their organization The Black Panther Party For Self-Defense.

There was an absolute leadership vacuum in America, black and white. Kennedy was dead and Johnson had caved in. Malcolm X was dead and Martin Luther King, Jr., did not have the ear of those who rebelled, set torches to

cities, and resorted to arms. It was into this breach that
the Black Panther Party stepped. There was no competi-
tion. There was not another single organization in America
with the winning combination that the Black Panther
Party had. The split was between those who ran and hid
under the bed and those who ran and hid in the woods.
The stuff had to be dealt with on the spot. Under the bed,
first of all, were all the politicians, doctors, lawyers, and
most of the teachers. The woods were full of folks who
wanted to be underground. They pledged themselves to
fight, for blackness, for black power, and black liberation.
But they bored so far underground that they never quite
made it to the fire on time. They were always arriving
just as the ambulances, fire trucks, and police cars were
driving away. You sort of got the impression that above
all they were dedicated to survival.

From the moment it walked onto the scene, the Black
Panther Party took control of the situation. It is important
to note that the Black Panther Party existed for one whole
year, from October 1966 to October 1967, before any shots
were fired between Panthers and Police. By the time those
first shots were fired, the Black Panther Party had already
captured the imagination of black America and was fast
on its way to becoming a national organization. A delegation from the Black Panther Party was recognized and
seated at the New Politics Convention held in Chicago in
1967. The Black Panther Party called for an end to the
spontaneous riots and uprisings. We knew that they were
not spontaneous. The better word for it was *unorganized*.
They were deliberate and willful, but unorganized. A poverty of imagination and a conscious desire to sugar-coat
the truth leads sociological minds to define such outbreaks
of violent behavior as spontaneous. If it is spontaneous,
then it is nobody's fault.

We knew that spontaneous violence was deliberate but

unorganized. It had to be harnessed, channeled, focused. It could not be controlled, any more than any other explosion can be controlled. Organized guns and force, is what Huey used to call the police, and he referred to the Black Panther Party as the organized guns and force of the black community. It was in that light that we wanted to be seen by black people. And I think that it was in that light that they saw us. We were their troops, Kamikaze if need be, in this hour of need.

Several attempts were made to hijack the Black Panther Party. The Sacramento confrontation is what did it. Television flashed the images of twenty-four Black Panthers in a delegation, armed with shotguns, rifles, and pistols, inside and outside the State House. An electric current snaked through black America. Thousands of people flocked to our banner, as a new expression and vision of their cause. They began to make the world over in the image of the Black Panther Party.

WHEN THE PANTHERS were arrested for their military hardware appearance on the California State House grounds in 1967 and for demonstrating inside the Assembly building itself at Sacramento, we faced enough charges to keep a law school busy for a semester. My parole officer and a host of other cops and helpers scanned the television films of the event for days, trying to spot me carrying firearms. They failed to do so because I hadn't been armed. Such a mistake would return me instantly to San Quentin. But they charged the whole group with indictments.

The Party was prepared to fight the State's case vigorously in court. During this period we were having hot conversations with two groups interested in our defense—the Communist Party and the Socialist Workers Party. Each group had a team of lawyers, but there was no way that we could get them together to figure out our best strategy. They were still busy arguing pro and con between Stalin and Trotsky, rehashing nitpicking points thirty years old. Our treasury was low, and we needed all the free legal types that we could find. The Socialist Workers Party became intolerable to communicate with, so we finally went with the Communists. That was our second mistake—the first, thinking that those two windbags could work with us, now that we were the establishment's target.

Wrong. Nor could we work with the Communist Party. When the District Attorney got specific, he wanted to nail Bobby Seale and two others. His plan was for them to plead guilty and take a ninety-day sentence in exchange for which the rest of the twenty-one who were in the Sacramento scenario would go free. "Nothing doing," we said. Seale and the other two had no police record to begin with —why nail them with a phony, plea-bargaining rap? Our Communist lawyers thought that the D.A.'s proposal was the greatest thing since marshmallows. To us, it was lousy. "You have to," they argued. "You have no alternative." On top of these tense discussions and the sweat-out we were having with the case, *these Communist Party lawyers hauled themselves off to Europe on vacation,* leaving us to stew and succumb in this awkward encounter with the government of California. The practical application of Karl Marx made us very bitter.

ALL AROUND THIS WORLD in my experiences with Communists and encounters with their teachings, I have suffered from their policies. Early on, in spite of the Cuban fiasco, it seemed that their activities in Asia and Africa would be flowingly positive and personally persuasive. During the four years that I headed the International Section of the Black Panther Party in Algiers, conference and speaking assignments took me into China, North Korea, North Vietnam, and much of the Third World. I spent several months in North Korea in 1970, during which time Kathleen had our second child. . . . Also long enough to become thoroughly disenchanted with their brand of communism.

At first I was amazed at the grit and zeal of the young Communists of North Korea. They were fanatical in their promotion of their premier, Comrade Kim Il Sung. Some of the most zealous had entered into a compact or vow that they would not marry or have sexual relations until their country was united with South Korea.

You could not say "Good Morning" or "Hello" to them without their responding: "Yes, it is a beautiful day, thanks to the inspired teaching of our beloved revolutionary leader, Comrade Kim Il Sung, who has filled our lives with the truths of Marxist-Leninist analysis and daily supports in our burdens and obligations—" That was good morning, and after six months it began to lose its novelty but not the power to bore.

In the days of my first excitement and enthusiasm for North Korea, I wrote to my Panther brothers in the United

States, urging the unification theme of Premier Kim Il
Sung and reflecting that

> after careful investigation of the international scene, it is
> our considered opinion that it is none other than Comrade
> Kim Il Sung who is brilliantly providing the most profound
> Marxist-Leninist analysis, strategy, and tactical method for
> the total destruction of imperialism and the liberation of
> oppressed peoples in our time.

What I didn't record was my increasing resentment over
the subtle brainwashing and unsubtle racism of the North
Koreans.

I was part of a delegation of journalists traveling under
Communist auspices throughout Asia. Beside myself, six
or seven of the two dozen writers were from North America. One was a young Chinese man from California, with
great enthusiasm for his ancestral homeland. Another was
a young radical Japanese woman from the West Coast,
really caught up in the righteous magic of this return to
Asia. She was hard-boiled, seldom smiled, and was always
most professional about her correct revolutionary stance.
The North Koreans took her apart.

The first week we were there, we were shown hours of
war movies and atrocity films, and we endured long lectures about the imperialism of America—and Japan. The
hatred for the Japanese was profound and endless. The
youngster from the West Coast caught it on both cheeks—
first for being Japanese, second for being American. The
Koreans were not friendly to her; they had limited capacity
to express the international solidarity of workers who were
supposedly united. Next that poor gal was ostracized by
the other women in our group. By the end of the tour, she
was ready for therapy or at least an exit visa from this
paradise of liberation and truth. The poison of racism hit
her where she least expected it; but then, that is the Communist style.

SEPT. 1948
FEB. 1949
NOT TRANSFERABLE

Above left: Eldridge Cleaver, age 13, student at Jordan High School, Watts, California. Right: Eldridge's father, Leroy Cleaver. Below: After father's absence of five years, he and Eldridge enjoy restaurant meal together in 1953.

Above and across opposite page: Prison mug shots. Photo in civilian clothes, taken at San Quentin, was one permitted to be sent to family after five years' imprisonment. Fifth and sixth photos in sequence show prisoner immediately after 1968 arrest in Oakland and as he appeared later after being permitted a shave and shower. Left: Identification cards. Eldridge was confirmed in the Roman Catholic faith while at Fred C. Nellis School for Boys, Whittier, California, his first time in reform school.

CLEAVER, LEROY ELDRIDGE

SELECTIVE SERVICE SYSTEM

NOTICE OF IDENTIFICATION

DEC 1 1953

Approval not required.

REFER TO YOUR SS NUMBER IN ALL COMMUNICATIONS ☞ | 4 | 111 | 35 | 266 |

You are a registrant with the local board indicated on the front of this card. The above is your selective service number. It identifies your State, your local board, your year of birth; and it identifies you among registrants of the same year of birth with this local board of jurisdiction. Copy this number in ink on the last blank line on the back of your Registration Certificate (SSS Form No. 2) and refer to it in any communications you may have regarding your selective service status.

The law requires you (1) to notify this local board of any change in your mailing address, (2) to notify it of any fact which might change your classification, and (3) to comply with all instructions received from this local board.

SSS Form No. 391
GPO 16—68052-1

Clara Haselke
(Signature of Local Board Member or Clerk)

Notice *of* Confirmation

Name	Leroy Cleaver
Father	Leroy Cleaver
Mother	Thelma Robinson
Date of Baptism	October 13, 1950
Church	St.Mary's Church, Whittier, Cal.
Confirmed by	Most Rev.Jos.T.McGucken, D.D.
Date	October 22, 1950
Sponsor	Mr.Morin Mieke

Eldridge Cleaver (wearing dark glasses) with Alprentice (Bunchy) Carter, founder of Los Angeles branch of Black Panther Party. Carter was killed in Los Angeles in January 1969.

Algiers. Left: Eldridge Cleaver in typical dress. Cloak was convenient for concealing arms. Center: Doors of Black Panther headquarters were under constant guard. Below: A time for special skills.

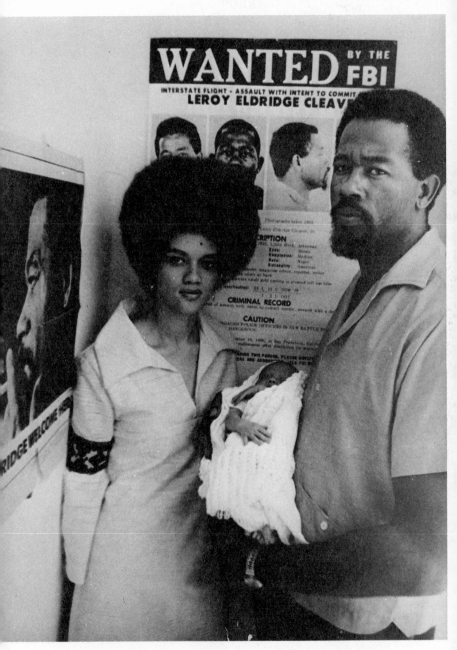

Algiers, 1968. Eldridge and Kathleen Cleaver with son, Maceo, one month old. Poster in background was Eldridge's "passport."

1970 tour by U.S. People's Anti-Imperialist Delegation visited No
Korea. Members view topographical model in Panmunjon (top) a
fortified bunker, now a museum exhibit, in Kaesong (below). To dest
bunker occupants, U.S. soldiers poured gasoline into entry and ignited

At Pyongyang, North Korea, Madame Kim Il Sung, wife of Premier Kim Il Sung, gave birthday party for Maceo Cleaver, one year old.

Algiers, 1972.
Joju Cleaver,
age one.

Above: North Vietnamese countryside. Bus carried delegation on their tour. Below: Undamaged Buddhist shrine in Hanoi.

*Above: Delegation poses with North Vietnamese General Giap.
Below: Hamrung bridge in North Vietnam was described to delegation as symbol of hope and defiance. Although obviously damaged, bridge was never knocked out.*

People's Republic of China. Above: Tan An-min Square in Peking. Below: Residents of old people's home, mostly 90- and 100-year-olds, enjoyed visit by delegation.

Top and center: Hanchow University scenes. 1970 tour of delegation included visit to home of Chinese cultural revolution and site of its beginning. Right: Inside Forbidden City.

The American Chinese gentleman would get his later—when we visited the Chinese wall, in fact. Here we gathered with all the drama and delight that affects foreign visitors. Our Chinese American visitor was in ecstasy; and after a long pause at a particularly lovely site, he spoke to our guide-interpreter in Chinese. She turned and glared at him; in words that cut to the bone, she said loudly, "Comrade Brother, please speak English. We cannot understand your version of Chinese." I put that incident down in my memory book, for it describes completely and simply Communist arrogance and insensitivity to the hopes and expressions of the human spirit.

For a long period I believed that the Communist system was the right alternative to the American political, economic, and social system that I had been battling in the States. I had taken fully the Marxist philosophy, with its attendant beliefs and doctrine, to be the answer to what I was looking for. (When you reject the American community, what do you buy? The Third World has no answers unless you love small-time dictators and police torture in the nearest precinct.) So I bought into Marxism, with its scientific interpretation of existence and its extreme criticism of all things religious. Anything pertaining to God was out. They hated the very idea of God.

Temporarily this worked well for me. I disliked religious professionals, priests, preachers—remember the clown that tore up the front of our house in East Los Angeles? He was exhibit number one. I believed that next to the politicians, preachers were the cause of much of our difficulties and the perpetuating of intolerable social conditions.

While I was inwardly chagrined at the coarse, racist manner of the overseas Communists, my greatest questioning was to develop in the area of religion. Here I had studied Communist ideology for twenty-two years, confident that I had mastered the philosophy. I wrote about it and taught others. In comparing the studies and witnessing the actual experience, however, I began to see through it.

Away from home, Marxism got very flaky. The most powerful, single breakthrough, in my Communist-held position, was the birth of my children. For me, each one was sort of a cosmic, spiritual event. A miracle . . . first, Maceo, and then my daughter. I didn't come out of the Marxist philosophy all at once. But this crack appeared like a breach in the wall—and the crack which never closed was the affirmation of life that gripped me at my children's birth and kept saying to me: here is a soul, here is a link in the chain of life.

Very carefully, communism had divided everything into materialism and idealism. Everything you couldn't measure or weigh, well, that was idealism, and therefore it didn't exist. Music, poetry, your soul, and everything that is related to religion was false. I had seen now in my own experience with my children that this was not true. And when that opening appeared, other questions followed and hastened the crumbling of the Communist intellectual empire.

Other circumstances confirmed these feelings, these inner doubts. In every Communist country I visited, I saw events and people and policies; and I would silently compare that reality with my memories of home. Quietly, America started winning. For every government practice I observed in Korea or China, I would think about how that worked out in the U.S.A. In Algeria, I had many months of this comparison game. For instance, when I saw someone arrested, I thought about the manner in which that happened. Or if I visited someone in prison, I would remember the contrast with San Quentin or Folsom. It was a begrudging process; and I would reflect that in America things just didn't happen that way; there were some principles, civilized procedures, due process. At the very least,

when someone was arrested, even during the terrible
months of 1968, you knew that a person would be heard
from in no more than 48 hours. At least you could call the
police department and get some information. In Algeria,
if you call the police, you'd better be calling from a pay
phone, if you can find one. In those other Communist
countries you never even talk about phoning the police
department. They play very rough over there and forget
about due process of law and the concept of innocent until
proved guilty—what a beautiful expression. But you don't
hear that in other places I've been.

Yes, I was a critic of the unsolved racial problems that
infected America; but there was something in me that said
I had to admit I was wrong in the way that I was looking
at America. And after Soviet Russia and viewing all these
Third World, third-rate dictatorships, I realized how special was our democratic form of government and the people that made it click. I was homesick and homeless.

7

BLOOD AND WINE
ARE RED

THE FINAL WEEKS in California before my exit to Cuba
were filled with public appearances, press interviews, and
invisible but frantic plans for escape. The inner circle of
the Panther organization knew that I would never return
to prison. In my eyes, that would be the equivalent to the
death sentence; and so it was my turn, for a short period,
to jump straight into a final shoot-out scenario. My plan
was to take over Merritt College in Oakland and turn it
into a fortress. It was an old two-story, concrete building,
complete with towers and a commanding view of the surrounding terrain. I wanted to hole up there with some fellow Panthers and tell the white power–police pig structure
to come and get me. We had plenty of military gear and

enough volunteers to join me in this action that would forestall my imprisonment, give me a fighting chance, and at least let me die outside of prison.

It was Huey Newton's turn to veto this death extravaganza. He sent orders from his cell that nothing of the sort was going to happen and notified the Central Committee that they should do everything possible to get me out of the country. His argument was sound and was followed. The Panthers had to have someone out of prison and out of the clutches of the death squads that were moving in on us all over America.

If we were going to sustain a revolutionary protest and program, it would have to come from the living; and this meant my going into exile. Cuba was our first choice. We did not suspect that the Cubans were playing a double game, that the rules had changed; and the opportunities in the Castro island seemed ideal in many ways. They were Communists, blacks had a share in the power, and they were close enough to America for a return of guerrilla forces. But how to get there?

When it was under discussion that I would flee California, jump bond, and head for the Caribbean, all kinds of plans were proposed. In the end, three or four made sense. One was to complete an invitation to speak in Knoxville, Tennessee; then hijack the plane leaving Knoxville, and fly to Cuba. But it was too desperate a move, conceived in desperation by a well-wisher who was much more uptight than I had ever been; and as the days marched on, the cover on my trail intensified. Police and FBI were everywhere—at restaurants, at interviews with the press, at student rallies, following me home, and planting certain black spies within the organization itself. I trusted no one but gave no outward sign of suspicion. Some staff people would take me aside and mention a super plan they had worked out for my escape. "Fine, fine," I would say confidentially to them. "Go ahead and work that out." I had four or five "confidential" plans being developed simultaneously and then, at the last minute, surprised them all with a really secret scheme that no one ever understood.

But before Tennessee came an appearance at Stanford, and that speech was a valedictory address: a long goodbye lecture. While it was not my last talk in America, it was the most organized and reflective during that tumultuous time.

The opening theme was aimed at the natural coalition of black and white radicals to confront the power structure that was strangling America. Some critics accused me of toadying to the rich white upper class students at Stanford. Wrong. I was not playing to their guilt level but to their participation energy that had been manifest in the anti-war, peace movement. Not a little of our money was coming from concerned white liberals who were shelling out for the Huey Newton Defense Fund and also had posted bail for me. These people were genuine, and I resented the attack that I was playing patty-cake with the whites. Besides, my feelings ran much deeper than that revolutionary moment. My mother had taught all her children that there were whites you could count on, for they were good and just, and that there were blacks you should avoid, for they were unkind and dishonest. Our family was not fed racism even though we all, at times, suffered from it. I argued this position night and day within the Panthers, particularly those who wanted to shoot every white person standing. Our claim was simple—we were against police brutality; and some of them were black, and they were the enemy as well as the white holsters. It was an argument that never failed and delivered us from the ultimate destruction, blacks becoming the very thing they were trying to eliminate, racists.

Being a black in white America is full of ironies. While

I was lecturing the Stanford crowd on their segregated churches and their residential housing patterns which excluded Negroes, plans were already in motion to hide me those last days in the apartments of college girls. I was doing my best to elude the glovelike surveillance the police had fastened on my activities in the Bay Area; and several students from Berkeley, young people who had attended my lectures and supported the Panther cause, were providing me with an urban refuge. The latest irony is that I am now, ten years later, a part of the Palo Alto Peninsula community. My children attend schools in that district; I work out of an office a few miles from Stanford and have been offered a teaching post there. That is the complexity and opportunity of America and reflects some of the possibilities today that appeared so unreal in 1968. I thank God for the changes in my life that made these happenings come about—and also the improvements and alterations that have touched our society in America to let these things develop. It is a brand new existence, like being born yesterday.

THE DAY BEFORE I WAS TO return to prison, a Panther colleague from Los Angeles slipped into town. My San Francisco residence had a carnival atmosphere, although there wasn't much laughter or celebration. Supporters were keeping a vigil on the front walk, carrying signs and chanting, "Keep Eldridge free," that Cleaver must not go to prison. A couple of squad cars constantly circled the block, others were parked at the curb with plain clothesmen checking out everybody's movement. Kathleen and I were in and out of the house that week, but I was staying away at night. The vigil of supporters and the surveillance of police was just too constant for sweet slumber.

General Omar Bradley once said that you had to have a plan in military operations to be successful. Even a bad plan was better than no plan, he argued. I was surrounded with escape plans. One group had me riding into the Rockies on horseback and then escaping to Canada. I was no Lewis and Clark operator, but I expressed interest in the deal. A couple of white sympathizers offered to hijack a jet (with hand grenades) and whisk me off to the islands. That was vetoed by everybody. Someone else had a private launch ready to make the dash to Cuba—I told them to stand by.

My personal plan worked because it was secret and out of the normal corridor of Panther activities. We were so saturated and infiltrated with government agents that I could not possibly trust even the so-called inner circle. (During the last week in California, I happened to look through the gun closet—a whole rack of rifles nicely in place. Each one had a belt of ammunition attached. Beautiful and ready. Only one problem—a little further checking revealed that none of the ammunition would fit the weapon to which it was attached! Like I said, we were full of double agents, and they were busy doing their thing.)

I told no one of the real plan—not even Kathleen—only what they needed to know. Except Ralph Smith from Los Angeles, and a white couple who were part of the Mime Troup.

Escape was a very trying act. On the last afternoon in San Francisco prior to being hauled away to San Quentin, Kathleen and I drove up to our house, pushed through the chanting demonstrators and stand-by police, and spoke a few words from the front porch. Then I went inside and there was Ralph Smith—a Panther who was a near double for me. In a moment, he and Kathleen returned to the front steps and continued the revolutionary rhetoric about not going to the pig prison. A couple of Panthers in the crowd were cued to ask "me" questions which Ralph answered in grand style. Whites say that all niggers look alike, and Ralph and I fit the bill for the watchful authorities. As they continued this charade, I went out the rear door and over the back fence into a waiting car that took me to where I prepared for stage two of my goodbye to America.

Rather carefully the Mime Troopers made me up to look like a sick old man. They sliced some hair off my head and put on a mustache. They put me in a baggy suit and shuffling shoes, and had me carrying an old briefcase under a black bowler hat. I wore thick glasses (which gave me an incredible headache) and did a lot of heavy breathing as we made our way into the San Francisco airport bound for JFK. Past security, past any questions or detention, this little old wheezing nigger was led by a young woman in white who urged the flight crew to give me special attention on the trip to New York. It was high drama, so effective that, en route, a stewardess even gave me a shot of oxygen—my breathing sounded a little shaky to her.

I had won. Here I was out of the clutches of the California courts, my wallet stuffed with $15,000 cash—a royalty check had just come from *Soul on Ice*—and I soon would be in sunny Cuba, setting up the big training camp while preparing to deal with Nixon's American Dream. Yet I was the one to be broken by the collapse of false dreams and faded illusions of revolutionary possibilities. After my connecting plane to Montreal and then a Cuban freighter ride—in a closet—to Castroland, I was to live six months in a wretched and restless existence—sort of a San Quentin with palm trees, an Alcatraz with sugar cane.

The Cubans kept me out of sight for almost a year before a Reuters wire story indicated that old Eldridge Cleaver was holding out in Havana. The Castro people denied our existence in their island paradise and gave me a new suit and a ticket for Algeria.

By then the disenchantment was mutual. The white Cubans were locking up all the Black Panthers, putting our hijacker friends in work camps, and increasing their general hostility toward me. (At one point it looked like we would have a shoot-out with their security police when I refused to turn over some machine guns in my Havana apartment.)

The Algerian sojourn started off on a bleak note. I claimed a rightful place in their diplomatic scene as head of the International Section of the Black Panther party. At first I was isolated in a dinky house along the Mediterranean, joined by Kathleen, our baby, and a couple of Panthers from the States. It was only through the successful promotion and sponsorship of the Vietcong, which soon became the Provisional Government of Vietnam, that we broke through to any recognition or status. As they up-graded their own situation (through the escalation of events in Vietnam and the negotiations in Paris), they told the Algerian government to let us have their old embassy quarters. It worked. Vietnamese were really well informed on what was going on inside America. For nearly three years we operated out of this residence on embassy row, complete with public rooms, apartments, communication office with Telex equipment, and a sense of power and place. We went to diplomatic receptions, entertained na-tional and foreign visitors, promoted all kinds of interna-tional intrigue, and were immensely satisfied with our power position in North Africa.

The Cuban disaster was still eating me. Castro lost a lot of friends in Europe and Africa after I got through telling our brothers overseas what a farce his program had be-come. I warned Africans to beware of this cigar store revolutionary, for I had seen the brutal accomplishments of his grand design. I had met others than those of the Communist Party, talked to people who were not military public relations experts, and witnessed the day-to-day life in a Communist Caribbean island. Yes, it's true that people were eating better than under Batista, that they held jobs and enjoyed improved housing; but even my thick skull could perceive and understand the new misery that sat-urated Castroland: the unrelieved suffering of mind and spirit that comes from living under a dictatorship. I passed this word back to Panthers in America and gave this warn-ing to black leaders in Africa who thought they could make use of Castro in their own liberation struggle. Be careful, I said, or you will trade in your old chains for new ones, and the new ones will be harder to break than the old.

8

ALGIERS

YOU MAY RECALL that Algiers was pushing to be the radical capital of the world. Their military government was cast in the most extreme socialist terms, such that they were constantly breathing threats against all white colonialist governments in Africa. They always wanted a new war with Israel, taunted the conservative Arab governments, and had a welcome mat for any besieged revolutionary in need of sanctuary. It was also a country in chaos, torn up by cultural and social conflict, reeking with poverty, and corroded with political intrigue.

Daily life in Algiers is something out of a Western movie. Everyone was armed. People were always disappearing in broad daylight. Women in veils peered out of upstairs windows like damsels in distress. Bribery, payoffs, blackmail, and smuggling were identifiable national goals. A ruthless, frequently violent, male chauvinist brotherhood ruled the country, with savage skullduggery and unwritten rules that one could hardly fathom. Trust and loyalty were unknown words. Money, power, and influence were about all that worked, and we survived for a while on that wavelength.

My presence got a big lift when the Pan African Cultural Festival had its first event in Algiers during the summer of 1969. It was sponsored by the Organizaton of African Unity, a 35-nation body that brought together some 4,000 participants including writers like myself, but also dancers, actors, artists, and musicians from all over the continent. It went on for nearly two weeks and gave me the opportunity to meet personally the top people of all the liberation and opposition movements in Africa, as well as representatives from eastern Europe and several Palestinian Liberation groups. During this late summer event, the Black Panthers opened the Afro-American Information Center in Algiers. Quite a few celebrities hopped over from Europe. Also, people like Stokely Carmichael and his singer wife, Miriam Makeba, made the scene. It was a good moment for me, for I now had a broad spectrum of international contacts.

I have mentioned the fact that I traveled extensively within the Red orbit while I was living in Algeria. In the next forty months, I visited Korea twice and China once. I spent nearly six weeks in North Vietnam and found those people to have the most refreshing attitude within the Communist bloc. The opposite, the most up-tight, were the Koreans. As for the Chinese, they seemed to be above it all, basking in their cultural self-confidence and in their age-old sense of place. For they did have a place where one could spend a lifetime in pursuing their art, architecture, music, food preparation, and world view. At times their world view is beyond comprehension.

They are going to survive. Right now they have prepared underground cities to function smoothly and safely if faced with atomic attack: I mean, complete underground systems of factories, shops, dormitories and schools, power plants, highways and hospitals—and, I suppose, collective farms. I remember during one visit to Pyongyang a Belgian economist and I were eating dinner at the same table with some Chinese state planners. The Chinese official was blowing the mind of the Belgian by explaining that *every* Chinese person is entitled to one egg a day—and describing the production and logistics of getting 700 million eggs to the table every morning. Then he turned to me and asked how many Negroes there were in the United States. I paused, wanting to make this look good, for we were playing an incredible mega-numbers game. The U.S. government used to say that there were 25 million blacks in the country. The Panther figure was 35 million—we wanted to have a power base, so we included the people who were passing as whites. But under these oriental circumstances, I said, "About 40 million blacks in America." The Chinese expert stared at me a minute and said quietly, "Ah, we have some villages that size."

By now the Panthers had adopted an Asian strategy in our relations with the Communists. While I personally had favored the unsmiling style of Joseph Stalin, the Russians were too messed up, living under the shame of being revisionists and hopelessly ensnared in double dealing with everybody, and we didn't want to link up with them. So the international wing of the Black Panther Party, which was essentially statements, speeches, and press releases, supported the "Asian strategy." The United States was the spearhead of imperialist aggression buried in the heart of Asia. The Korean people were serious in supporting us because they wanted the Americans out. The Chinese, the people of Mao's Little Red Book, were also serious in this opposition to American interests in the Far East. Of course, the Vietnamese were the most serious of all, for they were at war with the Americans. The Vietnamese were amazing—both in Algeria, where they became our most vigorous advocate with the Boumédienne regime, and in North Vietnam, where they were the most cordial, the most relaxed. It is a strange irony that the United States should be in conflict with the most progressive Communist element—the North Vietnamese—in a long military fiasco. Their historic, natural tension has always been with the Chinese, and during my visits, their deepest complaints were always directed toward China and Russia. At heart they were seeking independence from everyone—they had held China at bay; they had evicted those European tenants, the French; and now they were finally getting Uncle Sam off their backs.

In North Vietnam I had my closest, most intimate contacts with top leaders in the government—the party, and the military. I attended several briefings with General Giap during my Haiphong stay. He had made his reputation as Chief of Staff during the long French occupation, culminating with his grand siege and victory at Dien Bien Phu. He was brilliant, yet down to earth. He spoke about ten major languages. He used to say that you needed to learn the language of your enemies as well as your friends.

The Premier of North Vietnam, Pham Van Dong, personally welcomed our U.S. People's Anti-Imperialist Delegation that toured the North. At one reception he paid a personal tribute to me that I will never forget (and one reason why I feel that of all the Communist countries, I would still be welcome in his). He did a play on words of the French translation of my book, *Soul on Ice*. When they put you in an American jail, the slang expression is that you are "on ice." And the title of my book meant that my soul was in prison—in jail. The French have a different expression for the same experience—a person is not on ice, but he is "in the shadows" (out of the sun). The French title of my book translated *Un Noir a l'ombre*—"a black in the shadows." A notable poet in his own right, the premier understood this nuance in the foreign translation and said at this party, "In the West you are a black in the shadows, but here you are a black in the sun." That touched me deeply—both his awareness of my writing and his sensitivity to my difficulties in being in exile.

There is an old but true saying: your enemy's enemy is your friend. The North Vietnamese and the Vietcong were forever friends of the Black Panthers. In the United States, before my flight to Cuba, they were in regular touch with our movement, and were up to date, in considerable detail, on what was happening inside the U.S.A. All we knew of what went on in Vietnam came from them, and it wasn't much.

Recognition of the International Section of the Black Panther Party by these Asians gave me status and belonging in the overseas jungle. Without diplomatic recognition, I was simply a notorious gangster. While in Cuba I kept my sanity by stopping in almost weekly to visit at the Vietnamese and Chinese embassies. The confidence level with these people was something to behold. We learned that, in Cuba, they were prepared to give Panthers asylum should the Castro people rush us or hint at shutting down our apartment headquarters in Havana. This long-range foreign connection was our lifeblood. The State Department was constantly identifying me as a fugitive from justice, a roving hoodlum or something. They made every effort to lock a criminal identity to my speeches and activities; the Vietnamese not only lent credibility to my overseas operation but intervened on our behalf when the Algerians clamped down. And when the Algerians clamp down, I'm talking about a coffin lid, not a closed door.

THE FIRST MONTHS in Algeria saw this Panther and his family and a couple of wanderers living in a shack on the Mediterranean. I have noted that the Vietcong came to our rescue, passed on their villa to us when they were upgraded to diplomatic row, becoming the Provisional Government of South Vietnam, participating in the Paris peace conferences. Algeria was the base of operation for the Vietnamese delegation to Paris. There was a big hassle over this. The Black Liberation groups from South Africa, Angola, Mozambique all wanted this residence and made a lot of noise. But the Vietnamese saw the thing through, not backtracking, in the face of opposition as politicians do. To everyone's surprise, they turned over the villa to us and continued to sponsor us during the tightest moments with the Algerian government.

I always felt that we could take care of ourselves vis-à-vis rivals or enemies who wanted to get physical with us. We had fast cars, Russian machine guns, and plenty of fresh-air macho. But the Algerian government in its crooked dagger style of rubbing people out, very nearly reached us, and would have, had it not been for the Vietnamese and the North Koreans. Eventually there came a sprinting exit from Algiers to France. But first, let me describe the daily life of a Negro from America making it as a Panther minister in North Africa.

Housing we had secured, along with international recognition, right down to the Brass Wall Plaque. But we were broke. And the only way we could survive in this inflation factory was to start hustling for money. My criminal education in East Los Angeles helped us out significantly in North Africa. The first effort that paid off for us was trafficking in stolen passports and counterfeiting visas.

Being without an American passport overseas was like being paralyzed in a snake pit. As a visitor, the only place I could go was in the Communist bloc, and even then I had only a temporary visitor card. The United States did not have diplomatic relations with the Algerian government, so American interests were a subdivision of the Swiss, complete with state department types, office personnel, but no Marine guards. I was quite immune to any moves they might make in my direction; in fact, I got to know most of the people in Algeria who worked for the State Department and was always hassling them to get Secretary Rodgers to give me my passport. The reply was always very understanding and very "no," Washington was not going to give me a travel ticket. They would, I was later notified, guarantee my safe passage to the United States, should I want to return (and go to jail), but a regular passport would never be issued.

So I started issuing my own. After a season, the Americans in Algiers all knew each other, went to the same parties, attended the same open houses, shared the same swimming beaches, gas stations, and airport departure lounges. Several of the Panthers were dating personnel at the embassy, both American and Swiss, and we knew a lot about what was going on in that compound. And nationals of other countries passed on information to us they thought we could use. A lot of information arrived anonymously.

Before long a couple of the American office types had slipped some passport blanks out of the embassy, and we were in business creating our own travel documents. On one of my regular visits to the same American outpost, when people were distracted by another issue, I pocketed the seal of the State Department and tried it out on the material we had received. The Algerian authorities were embarrassed, and although they never accused us of swiping the seal, they let us know that they'd like to see it returned, with no questions asked. So after a while, I mailed the thing to the head of the Algerian police agency concerned, which had a name like Center for the Study of International Problems.

But leave it to the Germans. There were, and are, a lot of radical movements in Europe; and the Germans in the early seventies had their own brand of Weatherman and SDS. They were 1,000 percent in favor of the Panthers, wanted Americans out of Vietnam, and were heartily supportive of our Algerian enterprise. Through special contacts, some German scientists developed an advanced technique to assist us in our passport problem. (We learned that all the blanks were computer-coded, were easily traced as being unissued and stolen, and were of no use to anyone.) Other American passports, officially clean, could be used by myself and others if we could figure out a way to remove the photograph and put in our own without leaving a trace. That is an exotic process, almost like creating counterfeit money—all those little colored threads in the paper and the adhesive qualities of the process are unreal. But not to the Germans. They loved us and our cause plus the challenge of changing those passports with a unique, portable process that our people could learn. Portable meant that we could change passports right at an airport locker room, even use the same document for different people traveling—just keep changing the pictures.)

When we had mastered this skill, the production of visas was next. Visas are in great demand in Europe and North Africa, even from among government officials, as well as revolutionary leaders and all kinds of business promoters. By purchasing a fraudulent visa, the Europeans in Algiers could move in and out of the country without officialdom being aware of their furtive movements. Arabs were in a particularly delicate fix. They might want to return to Egypt or duck into Libya or fly over to Geneva or Zurich with a bagful of currency without the Algerian authorities knowing it. All those travelers want to go somewhere on a weekend or holiday, especially without the Algerians eyeing their motives or destination. Adept as we became at producing these travel visas, we made thousands of dollars for our expenses during that four-year stay.

We also used to run stolen cars from Europe. It was incredibly easy. Someone would rent, steal, purchase, or lease a car in Germany, England, Italy, Holland, etc., drive to Marseilles and take the boat ferry from there to Algiers. Cars we brought into Algeria found their way throughout the Third World. Once the cars arrived in North Africa, we would create new vehicle identification papers and sell the units to auto-hungry Arabs and Africans. Sometimes Panther sympathizers would simply put 10 percent down and never finish paying for the car that sat in one of our lots in Algiers. As for the Algerian government, they did not go out of their way to bother anybody—unless you caused trouble for them. No questions asked as long as you did not cross their invisible boundaries of law and *dis*order.

All of this criminal activity was not creating the brave new world that I hoped to establish overseas. I wanted to come home and made several attempts, on my terms, to gain readmission to the United States. But nothing developed. The necessity for so much hustling to keep the organization afloat was driving me back into gangster patterns that I thought I had left: the regular use or threat of firearms; the readiness for attack or a street corner shootout (the ambassadors of other countries drove around the city in protected cars, bristling with automatic weapons, grenades, and the equipment of military prowess), and the protection of oneself in a very tense society.

Besides the preservation of one's self and one's family, I had the supervision of nearly thirty other people in my command. And this assortment of revolutionaries, hijackers, bank robbers, and revolutionary Communists can force the leader in charge to become a very mean, authoritative honcho. More than once someone in our Algerian company would dispute my orders or challenge my leadership or do some dumb thing that would bring the Arabs to our residence with flags flying and armored cars rumbling in the driveway. The system, to the Arabs, was simple. I was in charge of the Panthers. Anytime one of our people got out of line, I was to inflict punishment and state that it would never happen again. And these confrontations with my own people were often at gunpoint.

There were times in Algiers when the more cutthroat types within the Panthers wanted to do something dramatic, like shoot up the American diplomatic professionals or, at least, kidnap the top official, Ambassador Thomas Eagleton. We became acquainted with Mr. Eagleton and had frequent conversations during my Algerian stay. I enforced a hands-off attitude to the gunpowder terrorists who were always scheming some major disaster. I told them that good relationships, even with our enemies, was necessary for survival in the world. Nothing would be accomplished by vamping on the American staff.

BY EARLY 1972 the radical quotient of Algiers was getting saturated. Bernadine Dorn, on the most wanted list of the FBI, was rumored to be in North Africa—actually, it was her sister, Jenifer—and we played up her visit. Abby Hoffman's wife drifted through, plus a series of some very aggressive hijackers, who wheeled in in a Delta jet from Florida and caused a global commotion, to say the least. These Panther sympathizers came in great style—even had a million and a half dollar ransom intact. We thought this should be delivered, along with the hijackers, to our headquarters. "No," said the Algerians. They would take care of the details and ended up returning the money.

We felt absolutely betrayed but not surprised. The Algerians had been bluffed out of their revolutionary stance and were leaning toward establishment diplomacy with the United States, which certainly did not improve our situation. Great anxiety developed over the hijacked jets, the money, and the new direction of the Algerians, which became very hostile toward me in particular and the Panthers in general. I wanted to make sure that everybody knew what was going on behind the scenes, so I issued a worldwide open letter to President Boumédienne. Such a brash and public statement was shocking to the Arab community and outright dangerous in Algiers.

If I didn't know before, I soon understood that Islam is basically theocratic, and the chief of state stands next to Allah. It was regarded as humiliating for a foreign guest to address the chief of state in this manner; but I did, and I believe it saved our skins—particularly mine. Normal Algerian procedure would have been to help me to disappear, in the ocean or desert. I could see that developing and decided to take the public route so other people would be alert to the conflict between the Panthers and the Algerians.

REVOLUTIONARY PEOPLES   B.P. 118—GRANDE POSTE
COMMUNICATIONS NETWORK   ALGER—ALGERIE
                                             TELEPHONE 78 21 05
                                             TELEX 91905 RPCN ALGER

International Section Black Panther Party

Algiers, August 2, 1972

An open letter to:

His Excellency Houari Boumédienne
President of the Council of the Revolution
Algerian Democratic and Popular Republic

Dear Comrade Boumédienne,

During the struggle of Algeria for its national liberation, you lived, both inside and outside your country, under the constant threat of death because of your uncompromising revolutionary activities on behalf of your people. You have therefore become an authority on the vicissitudes in store for those who undertake the arduous task of struggle against the system of oppression.

Recently, I had the pleasure of watching, on television, your triumphal return to Tunisia, the site of many of your activities for the liberation of the Algerian people. And I got the impression that you had gone full circle. History records few such cases of a hunted man struggling against great odds, living continually with the threat of execution, who has then been able to make a triumphal return to that same country at the head of the government of his people.

It is because of your personal experience in struggle, the privation and opposition which you suffered, and your dedicated perseverance to final victory, that I am addressing this letter to you, with full confidence that you are equipped by experience to understand, and with hope that you are inclined, as befits a revolutionary warrior for the liberation of his people, to be sympathetic towards those who are still locked in the struggle for the liberation of their people.

I trust that you will not be offended by my making this an open letter to you, because no offense is intended. My main reason for making this an open letter is that at least I can be assured that it will come to your attention, which is something I cannot say with the same confidence about my other attempts to communicate with you recently. Indeed, the members of the International Section of the Black Panther Party find it almost impossible, these days, to communicate with any member of the Algerian Government, with the exception of those at the very lowest levels who have no information, and who are unable to resolve even the most trivial problem. But beyond these considerations, and perhaps most importantly of all, the recent developments, involving the Algerian Government, the Government of the United States, the International Section of the Black Panther Party, and the Afro-American Liberation Struggle, pose a number of questions to which many people in the world require, demand and deserve answers.

The establishment of the International Section of the Black Panther Party, which was officially opened on Sep-

tember 13, 1970, was an historic advancement for the
Afro-American Liberation Struggle. This marked the first
time in the history of the Afro-American people that we
were able to consolidate a foothold on the international
level, in a friendly country whose valiant people waged a
heroic war of liberation from French colonialism. It
marked the first time in history that Afro-American Freedom Fighters succeeded in establishing machinery to serve
the struggle of our people, beyond the reach of the forces
of the United States ruling class.

The Afro-American people are a people of African
descent, whose forefathers were kidnapped by slave-
traders, uprooted from our ancestral Motherland of Africa,
and cast down into the bottomless pit of inhuman slavery
in the United States of America. So that it was with a
triumphal spirit of "homecoming," of return to Africa,
that we undertook the establishment of the International
Section of the Black Panther Party. We felt that a vital link
had been forged, that we were amongst our brothers and
sisters of Africa, and that from this small beginning we
could build a mighty unity between our people . . . and
our brothers and sisters in Africa who are struggling for a
world of freedom and peace, in which all the children of
Africa can enjoy the fruits of a life consistent with the
precepts of Human Dignity.

The Afro-American people will always be grateful, and
we will never forget, that the Algerian people and government, and you personally, President Boumédienne, extended to our struggle this helping hand in our hour of
need.

The Afro-American people are fully determined to carry
out our struggle, from brutal racist oppression and exploitation, until final victory. Nothing can weaken this
resolve in the least, for if we were to compromise our
struggle at any point, it would be a betrayal of the blood of

our people, spilled in torrents over four hundred years, and a sacrifice of the future, bequeathing to our children the chains that now bind us. This we shall not do.

In concrete terms, this means that we shall continue to fight—using every means available to us, which we judge to be in the interest of our struggle and consistent with revolutionary principles. We believe that our struggle is a profound contribution to the struggles of the other oppressed people of the world, and to the independent countries of the Third World, that are struggling to free themselves from the new yoke of neo-colonialism. . . .

The Afro-American people fully recognize that this is their historic moment of opportunity to strike a final blow for their complete freedom. And we shall not hesitate.

When it comes to the specific questions of the expropriation of American airplanes by American revolutionaries and freedom fighters, we feel, first of all, that it is an internal problem between the American people themselves, to be settled by them, and not by others who are only incidentally involved. However, for purposes of discussion, the most important point that should be raised—a point which the United States Government goes to great lengths to obscure—is, why is it that the American people have resorted to this desperate measure? What is going on inside the United States that spurs the sons and daughters of America, and lately entire families and combinations of families, to take this fundamental step? It is the unbearable pressure of oppression, and the high, dedicated resolve of those who are struggling to put an end to the racism, savage, inhuman atrocities and cold-blooded exploitation that gives birth to this act.

To carry out our struggle for the liberation of our people, as any and every revolutionary and freedom fighter fully understands, we must have money. There are no ifs, ands, or buts about that point. Without money to organize

and finance the struggle there will be no freedom, and
those who deprive us of this finance are depriving us of
our freedom. This is clear. It is for this reason, and this
reason alone, and not because of any humanitarian considerations, that the ruling circles of the United States are
going crazy over the prospects of the one million and a
half dollars recently expropriated by these American
revolutionaries and freedom fighters, coming into the
hands of the International Section of the Black Panther
Party. . . .

The Afro-American people are not asking the Algerian
people to fight our battles for us. What we are asking is
that the Algerian government not fight the battles of the
American government for the ruling circles that are op-
pressing the whole of the American people. . . .

American revolutionaries and freedom fighters do not
come to Algeria begging, but rather we came to Algeria
because we knew that Algeria understood and respected
the rights of oppressed people who are struggling and
fighting for their liberation. In the past, during Algeria's
war for national liberation, Algerian revolutionaries and
freedom fighters had to turn to others for the assistance
and aid which they needed, deserved and received. . . .
I know that Algeria understands the value of assistance
and support given to oppressed people as they carry out
their struggle for their freedom and liberation.

Finally, I would like to say that I understand the pressure which the United States government is able to bring
to bear, to force people to knuckle under to its demands.
But this pressure must be resisted. To give in to it will only
feed its greed in its lust to compromise others and suck
them into the pit of reaction in which it has trapped itself
by its own deeds and actions. In humbleness, and in all sin-
cerity, I think that it would be consistent with Algeria's
traditions of struggle and revolutionary principles to con-

tinue welcoming American revolutionaries and Afro-American freedom fighters, whether they come to your shores—or your airfields—penniless or with millions of dollars, because it all goes to build the world of our dreams. Also, Algeria should demand that other African countries do likewise, because it is a part of Africa—the Afro-American people—who are asking you for this help, and to not let it be said that Algeria has turned its back on the struggle of the Afro-American people.

ALL POWER TO THE PEOPLE

Signed: Eldridge Cleaver

THE FOLLOWING IS the record of a conversation with Si Salah, Algerian head of *Renseignement Général*, the second division of the Algerian Political Police, roughly equivalent to the FBI, with their *Sécurité Militaire*, roughly paralleling the CIA. Present were Kathleen, Ronnie,* and myself. Si Salah had spoken in French, and Kathleen had interpreted. A strained meeting, it typified the precarious state of our existence and presaged our inevitable departure in search of a more hospitable climate for our activities. Si Salah had led the raid on our villa. It was he who had stood before our gate waving the search warrant above his head. That our case had been turned over to Si Salah was the worst kind of news. As was our custom, after the meeting, Kathleen went straight to a typewriter and wrote down every word she remembered, after which I added my recollections. Here is what remains.

Second Meeting with Si Salah
Wednesday A.M./16 August 1972

Yesterday, plainclothes police officers visited El Biar headquarters with a summons for Eldridge Cleaver. When Terry ** and Ronnie went down to the police station, they were told it was too late, to come back tomorrow

---

* One of our group of Black Panthers, name changed.

** Terry, as well as Bea, mentioned in the next paragraph, was another of our group. Their names have been changed.

morning. Eldridge also went to the police station, but
arrived after Ronnie and Terry had left.

This morning, about 10:00 A.M., Eldridge and I drove up
to El Biar * and a plainclothes police officer was standing at the gate. He asked Bea for Cleaver, and Eldridge
told him that he was Cleaver. He asked him if he had received the summons, and Eldridge told him yes, that we
were on our way down to the police station. He said that
he would go ahead, and got back into his car and pulled
off. We drove down to the chicken store and picked up
Ronnie, then to the post office where Kathy was mailing
some letters and told her to go back to the office and stay
there with Bea.

We got down to the police headquarters, and were told
to go to the second floor, where we had to wait, like the
last time Eldridge received a summons from Si Salah over
press releases, for over an hour. Finally, we were taken by
a uniformed police officer up to the sixth floor, into Si
Salah's wood-paneled, wall-to-wall-carpeted office.

We all sat down around the glass top table in Si Salah's
office and he proceeded to say that he had been informed
that we were planning to hold a press conference Friday,
and that that was forbidden. We asked him where did he
learn of such a press conference, that we had announced
only that on Friday, August 18, on the day designated by
OSPAAL ** as the International Day of Solidarity with the
Afro-American People, we were holding a ceremony at an
open house at our office. He said that that was all right,
that was symbolic, and there was nothing wrong with that.
We informed him that the press was aware of this, and
that we anticipated the press to come, and that we in-

---

* Section of Algiers in which foreign embassies are located.

** Organization of Solidarity of Peoples of Africa, Asia, and Latin
America.

tended to make a statement analyzing our liberation struggle and the revolutionary movement in the world.

Eldridge showed him the invitation that we had sent out
showing him what we had planned for Friday, August 18,
clearly showing that no press conference was involved.
Then he stated that he would, however, like to meet with
some political official and have the opportunity to discuss
the open house in order to prevent a recurrence of the
last raid on our office.

Si Salah began talking about how we were among the
twenty-five liberation movements recognized by Algeria,
and that we were viewed as a liberation movement, and
that our being allowed to function here increased our
credibility and we should be glad. But, that in this last
affair, we had gone beyond our prerogatives as a liberation
movement and began to operate as a state within a state.
That the matter of the hijacking was an internal affair
of Algeria, and that, in so many words, we had nothing to
say about it, and to take a position on it borders on interfering with the internal affairs of Algeria. Eldridge told
him that all the liberation movements in Algiers were dis-
satisfied, and that they all supported our position on the
money, but that they were afraid to say anything to him,
because he was the policeman.

Si Salah said that we could do anything we wanted to in
our own national territory—steal, murder, anything—but
once it came into Algeria, it was the affair of the Algerian
government. To get money for our struggle, we would have
to confine our robberies and ransoming to our own land,
and not take it outside. He said that the airline company
gave the ransom money to the hijackers for humanitarian
reasons, for concern over the lives of the women and
children who were on the plane, and for Algeria to accept
the money is to be an accomplice in that ransom. He said
that no government can act or has acted in that manner

Ronnie told him that was not true, because we have clippings from the newspaper showing where the Popular Front for the Liberation of Palestine held planes for five million dollars ransom and received it. They have used planes for ransom to get prisoners released, as they did when they demanded the release of Leila Khaled, and the governments released them for humanitarian reasons, for concern over the lives of the women and children held in the plane.

Si Salah said at one point that he was not a cop (gendarme) but that circumstances had forced him into this position because it was necessary; that he had lived the life that we are living; that he has been hungry, barefoot, and in exile; but that what kept him going was the belief in liberty. He told us that he had been in prison in Morocco, in prison in Tunisia, and that he did not hold it against the Moroccans or the Tunisians for putting him in prison, because they had their own interest.

Eldridge asked him if he liked it, and he said no, he didn't like it, and then Eldridge said that we didn't like it either. Si Salah said that he didn't like it, but he just took it as a further experience.

He began to talk about how if you want someone to give you something that they have, you have to study whether or not their own interests will be compromised by giving it to you; you cannot just stand there demanding that it be given to you, without some mutual understanding.

Eldridge told him that we agreed with him but that the Algerian authorities had blocked all our efforts to discuss the matter with them, that today was the first time we have been able to have any discussion whatsoever on the issue of ransom, and that the governing authorities had completely ignored us and our interest in the matter and made it impossible to discuss anything with them, over our requests.

Eldridge told him that it was the Algerian government that has created the problem by acting as if the hijacking was a matter of concern only to Algeria, and that by placing their national interests above the interest of an oppressed people, and acting as if their interests were the only interests that counted, they created the problem by refusing to discuss it with other people who were interested. Eldridge stated that there was no way to regard the matter as solely a concern of Algeria, for the airplane was hijacked in the United States, by Afro-Americans, and the money was taken off in the United States. Si Salah said that the only matter of concern for us was the participants.

He said that we understand that the last time an airplane was hijacked to Algeria, the Algerian government made restitution of the money to the Americans, and that the two hijackers were given political asylum here, above all the protests and boycotts of the airline associations. Implying, as he had in all previous interviews, that the same pattern would be followed this time.

Eldridge told him that it was only the imperialists trying to put pressure on Algeria that were involved with the boycott, and that there were many countries who would not go along with the boycott, and that Algeria should withstand the pressure and stick to her revolutionary principles. The only thing the Americans can do is wolf and make a lot of noise about it, but in the final analysis they will have to back off, because there is nothing they can do to harm Algeria. It is the Americans who have a need for the natural gas.

At that point Si Salah said that this is Algeria's gas, and we can sell it to whoever we like—capitalist, communist, it doesn't make any difference.

Then Si Salah began to talk about the Open Letter to Boumédienne, and how that was a bad tactic. He said that, in his personal opinion, in the first place, the letter was too long. It should have been one page, for it serves no purpose to talk on and on at length about something that could be said in a few words. In the second place, it was poorly written, and it wasn't addressed to anybody; it was sent to the President and ended with waiting for an answer. And, what was the worst thing of all, it became a tract distributed to all the press and media all over the world before it was sent to the President.

At that point, I told him that was totally incorrect because I had personally delivered it to the *Présidence*,* and I know when it was delivered. Eldridge told him that it was within the *Présidence* that the letter was delayed, and that he knew who did it. Si Salah got very uptight, and demanded to know who did it. Eldridge told him that he didn't trust him and wouldn't tell him, because it might be a good friend of his. Si Salah said it didn't matter if it was his brother, he wanted to know.

He told us that we should be thankful that the Algerian government allowed us to live here in exile, to function openly, and to receive enough money to operate. Eldridge told him that we were very grateful for that, and we always thanked the Algerians for that privilege, but that just having an office and the ability to function openly and the receiving of the *permanence* ** were not enough for us, that there were many things we had to do and we could not do them effectively in this manner and that we needed to have large sums of money to take care of business. Ronnie mentioned how one of our leading military comrades was in prison, and if we had the right kind of money we could liberate him from prison, like the Palestinians liberated Leila Khaled.

---

* The official residence of the President, comparable to the White House.

** A monthly financial allotment provided by the Algerian government.

Si Salah told us then that he was going to be perfectly frank with us, and tell us what is *believed:* that we don't do anything; we are nothing but Palace Revolutionaries.

Eldridge told him that we were being blocked from doing anything by the action of the Algerians, and that this is not the way we normally function, but we are the victims of their heavy blocking. Salah asked how long we had been blocked, and Eldridge said that it had been going on for quite a while, not since we first got here, but for quite a while now. He told them that it was obvious that they were blocking us, because in the case at hand we are confronting a political problem, and they have turned it over to the police as if it were a police problem, and it is not. We told him that we would like to be able to speak to someone else, because it was obvious that he had no respect for us, and no understanding of what was going on in the United States, and that we would get nowhere talking to him, and that we needed to be able to discuss with someone our preparations for leaving Algeria.

Si Salah said that we were too materialistic, that the problem was not money but that our people were asleep— that we needed to wake them up and then we wouldn't have any more problems. He agreed that it was not a matter for the police, that he represented a police power and not a political power, and that we should be able to discuss the problems and clarify our position once and for all with the political officials. But he disagreed that he didn't respect us, and began to run down all the cases he had on us. He started saying that for three years he has received reports that we smoke marijuana, and that we can't say that it isn't true.

Eldridge told him that we were fully aware of the plots that they were hatching to set us up for a drug bust, that we were aware of the threats they were making against friends who work closely with us, and the efforts

they were making to get them to say certain things
against us, and that we were not going for that. And that
we needed to talk to someone with some sense.

Si Salah then began waving his fingers in my face saying
that he has three complaints on Cleaver over a two-year
period for kidnap and death threats. . . . Salah stated
that although he was afraid of the family from whom
he had received the complaints, he didn't do anything, he
didn't come to our house, he didn't call us to his office,
he didn't make any moves, and, in fact, he stated on his
honor, that before the raid on our office he didn't even
know where we lived. Isn't that true? Although he has
received reports for three years about our using drugs, he
never made any moves against us. . . .

At one point in the conversation, Salah had mentioned
that two years ago he had sent in a request for Eldridge
to be expelled from Algeria, based on his behavior. He told
Eldridge, "I have never met you before that day you came
in my office, and I had never been to your house, but
from the reports I have received, I know you from the
top of your head to the tips of your toes."

We all laughed at that, and Eldridge told him that many
people around the world say all kinds of things about
him but that doesn't make them true. . . .

Ronnie told him that we would like to repeat very
seriously our desire to have discussions with the proper
authorities on receiving enough money for us to be able to
leave Algeria. Si Salah asked, "You want to leave Algeria?
Where will you go?"

Eldridge told him that we would have to leave Algeria
because we could not function in the manner that they
have designated for us. He told him that when they came
up to our office with their machine guns, they were trying
to provoke us into a shootout, and that we cannot relate
to that kind of treatment, we would have to leave here.

Si Salah began by saying that there was no kind of

provocation intended, that that was a strictly routine operation, that it happens all the time, but perhaps it was the first time that it happened to us so we were upset.

I told him it wasn't the first time that it had happened to us, that it happens to us all the time in the United States, that is how we were treated there.

Then Eldridge reminded him that we had to discuss with some political official also about the event for the 18th because we did not want there to be any misunderstandings, and we had to do it before the 18th. Si Salah said, yes, of course, before the 18th.

Then Ronnie reiterated that we also would like to talk to someone about the financial problem of leaving Algeria. In reply to Si Salah's question as to where we would go, Ronnie told him, "We're going back to Babylon to fight our war. We're not afraid, we're not afraid of anything. The death by a thousand cuts doesn't scare us. We are revolutionaries."

Si Salah said he would do what he could to arrange that. He again told us that he had lived the life we are living, he knows the importance of exile, he has been in exile, and he can understand us.

Eldridge then told him that the gun which they took during the raid was a personal gift to him from the Political Commissar of the People's Army in the People's Republic of the Congo, given to him by Ange Diawara during his visit to the Congo. And then Si Salah told him that they would return it.

Ronnie then asked him about the problem of having our telephone restored and our Telex turned back on, and Si Salah said he would do what was necessary to see that they were turned back on.

As we were leaving, Si Salah said something in Arabic to Eldridge, then in French, "You're hard-headed, you have a hard head." And Eldridge replied, "Yes, against the imperialists, not against friends." Si Salah said, "Well, regardless of what happens, remember that you are in a brother country."

I did not like the idea of Si Salah lecturing me on morality. I knew too much about him, and the things he had done as an FLN (National Liberation Front) militant. A legendary hit man, he had earned the nickname Salah Vespa following his successful escape on a motor scooter of that name, Vespa, after an assassination. Salah Vespa had been underground in France during the toughest period of the war, when civil war's sparks had spread from the French colonials in Algeria, Morocco, and Tunisia into the streets of Paris, Marseilles, and Lyon. He had the distinction of being one of the few Algerians for whom the French police refused to cancel arrest warrants, even though the war had long since ended.

Si Salah had done robberies and murders in the name of the Algerian War of National Liberation, and he had done these things in many countries of the world. He was a perfect example of the transformation of a revolutionary into a member of the new establishment. The gulf between us loomed up like the swallow of death. We were Outlaws and Inlaws starring at each other across our conflicting self-interest. He was the Outlaw become Inlaw, while I was an Outlaw still Out. The gap could not be bridged. One had to pass over to the other side, and the traffic ran up and down a two way street. A book I used to admire was entitled *From Prison to Power.** It told the common story of many men who had suffered imprisonment for their political beliefs and activity, men who had gone on to achieve supreme power in their lands, such as Nehru, Sukarno,

---

* Emil Lengyel (Chicago: Follett Publishing Co.).

Nkrumah, and many others. There was a need for a sequel
to tell the story of what happened to these men after they
got the power in their hands. One of the things they did
was to become Chief of Police, like Si Salah, who was now
finding himself in the position of policing the same kind of
behavior that got him his job.

Paris, 1974.
Eldridge Cleaver
at work in study of
Rue Bruant
apartment.

Joju and Maceo Cleaver (second row, second and third
from left) on school outing to French countryside.

Preparing to surrender. Above: Eldridge and Kathleen Cleaver accompany lawyer Karl Salans to American embassy in Paris. (Salans carried out negotiations with U.S. government.) Left: Inside embassy, ready to sign formal documents of surrender.

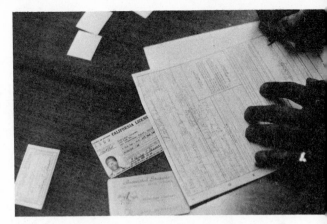

After signing of surrender documents (above) and flight to New York's Kennedy Airport, Eldridge Cleaver is flanked by two FBI agents for his return to California and further imprisonment.

San Francisco, 1976. At her apartment, Kathleen Cleaver and children prepare for visit to Eldridge at Alameda County Jail. Right: Joju and Maceo outside jail.

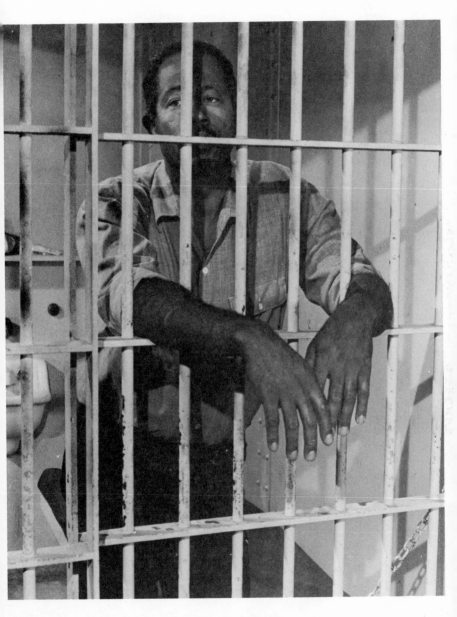

Scene from Gospel Films production, The Eldridge Cleaver Story.

Eldridge Cleaver meets the press. Above: Press conference immediately after release from Alameda County Jail, Friday, August 13, 1976. Below: On the well-known television show, August 29, 1976.

Above: Eldridge Cleaver with Senator Frank Church at Impact Symposium, Vanderbilt University, Nashville, Tennessee, April 1977. Both took part in program. Below: With Rev. Ralph Wilkerson and Charles Colson at Charismatic Clinic at Melodyland Christian Center, Anaheim, California, August 1977.

SHERATON PALACE

San Francisco, 1977.
Eldridge Cleaver
addresses National
Convention of
Black Evangelical
Association.
Below: Pasadena, 1977.
Joju, Kathleen,
Eldridge, and Maceo
Cleaver.

Above:
At St. Stephen's
Church of God
in Christ, San
Diego, May 1977.
Below and left:
At Chico High
School, Chico,
California,
giving testimony
and meeting with
audience, June 1977.

*Maceo, Joju, Eldridge, and Kathleen Cleaver with Eldridge's
mother, Thelma Cleaver, at her home in Pasadena,
August 1976.*

I had traveled throughout Europe under false papers and decided to live in France while friends worked for an official status that would permit me to stay. For awhile I considered Scandinavia—I had visited Sweden several times and felt comfortable with their anti-war movement. They had become a haven for army deserters and draft dodgers, with a real concentration around Stockholm. However, a Negro blends easily into the cosmopolitan aura of France, and I felt welcome in the political climate of Paris. Everyone was there, and every revolutionary body in the world seemed represented. Even the Palestinians and Israelis adjusted to each other's existence. Paris was loaded with anti-American rhetoric. France had lost its shirt in Vietnam and was now gratified to see Uncle Sam lose his pants. People in various movements agitated for my acceptance, and in August of 1972 I took up residence in Paris and proceeded to make myself at home. As it turned out, I was to spend some three years there, and my inner restlessness and spiritual emptiness were to reach awful proportions.

9

FINDING GOD—
FINDING ELDRIDGE

MY FAMILY—Kathleen, with our daughter and son, Joju, five, and Maceo, six—were with me in Paris. We had a house in the 13th Arrondissement, off the Boulevard de la Gare, at 9 Rue Bruant, at Metro Station Chevaleret. Our home was located directly across the street from the rear entrance of Hôpital Salpêtrière, one of France's finest. In perfect reflection of the symbiotic relation of life and death, reflecting also French efficacy and shortage of space, a mortuary was located a few yards away from the hospital rear gate. Ambulances entered the hospital in a steady stream, and the mortuary was the site for funerals all day long. Visitors of loved ones who were patients there cast a wary eye at the mortuary as they entered and exited the

hospital. If a hearse happened by, visitors seemed either
to visibly shrivel up and quicken their pace, or stop dead in
their tracks and stare after the hearse for awhile.

Our house, even at the exorbitant price of 1700 francs
(about $400) per month, was a bargain by Parisian stand-
ards. An ancient two-story structure, it had three large
rooms upstairs, laid out end to end. The one in the middle
was our bedroom, and the kids shared one room in which
we installed bunk beds. The third room was my study, in
which I spent the better part of a year, staring out the
window at the hospital gate, watching life and death go by
in an endless parade.

There were two large rooms downstairs—a long, narrow
kitchen, and off that a laundry room which converted instantly into a darkroom and in which were prepared the
false passports and identification papers I needed to survive. Kathleen's desk was heavy with a collage of books,
boxes, filing trays, and a typewriter, in one room where
she did her thing. The largest room, with a wonderful,
huge fireplace, contained our TV and was where we really
lived as a family. It was here, in this room, that I got to
know my children again after having been separated from
them for a year.

When the sky began to fall on us in Algeria and we knew
that our days there were numbered, the first thing we did
was to place our children with a wonderful Christian couple in New Jersey, whom I've never had the pleasure of
meeting, but to whom I am humbly grateful for the love
and shelter they provided Maceo and Joju during the most
treacherous period of our exile. I had slipped out of Algeria alone, leaving Kathleen behind, and was reunited
with her in Paris. Eventually we found this house and
when we felt secure with a network of friends and support,
we sent for the kids.

Outside, we had a large garage and an enclosed courtyard formed by the rectangular lay of the buildings around it. We shared the courtyard with five different businesses that were located elsewhere and used these buildings for warehousing their merchandise. During working days, they fetched merchandise back and forth in trucks. Otherwise, we had the whole place to ourselves. It was wonderful for the kids. They progressed from tricycles to bicycles in that courtyard. I bought a set of swings from le Bazar de l'Hotel de Ville, which I erected for them to play on. During inclement weather, I'd move the swings inside the long, cavelike garage. Since we had no car of our own, the garage became a playhouse for the children and a workroom for me, where I sawed and chopped wood for the fireplace, and dilly-dallied with bric-a-brac, as is my pleasure.

Paris is an apartment city, with space at a premium and our French friends would bring their children over to play in our yard, particularly on holidays and weekends. Maceo and Joju were always glad for someone to play with. Paris was bleak and depressing to them at first, particularly since they had to spend so much time inside the house because I was in hiding. In New Jersey, they had spent lots of time on a farm, with horses, dogs, rabbits, chickens, and ducks. And there was a tree back there which Maceo had ambitions of climbing some day. But in Paris there were no trees for him to climb, certainly not at our place; and in the public parks, such as the Luxembourg, it was a crime even to walk on the grass, which is there to look at, a backdrop for the Parisian tourist traffic to pose against for photographs.

When, in 1973, Kathleen had found the house, she thought it was perfect. When I saw it, I agreed. The heavy pedestrian traffic between the Metro station and the hospital, including workers, patients, and visitors, provided a perfect atmosphere of anonymity, ideal for someone living illegally in Paris, with a false I.D. and an assumed name.

Many of the workers, patients, and visitors at the hospital were black—immigrants from former French African colonies, most of them French citizens. Among the passers-by were Arabs and many French citizens from Martinique, now officially a part of France. Some of the people of color who passed my house were of a polyglot mixture that defied all classification, the results of hundreds of years of French colonialism and the march of French armies around the globe. You could meet anything there and no one took a second look. I was just another *noir*.

WITH SO MUCH delicate political intrigue in France, the French police were not to be toyed with. They took a very dim view of tampering with travel papers, visas, and passports, so my situation was precarious, to say the least. In spite of my anonymity, I was living in Paris without official clearance.

But I'd gotten lucky, and a mutual friend, Martine, had brought me to Fanchon's atelier. Even at that first meeting, I knew that Fanchon was something very special—a true angel of mercy.

When I came into the room, I didn't know that Fanchon's closest friend had just died. He had been a photographer in Saigon when cancer hit him, hard, and he began to wither away quickly. He was an American, but he left Saigon and came to Paris, to die—not so much to Paris as to Fanchon—and she was still profoundly shaken. I had just sort of plopped down, collapsed on the floor cushions, and leaned back against the wall. Fanchon's eyes widened into huge, white, staring discs. It was almost as if she was trying to hypnotize me, and I wondered what I'd gotten myself into. Martine had said only, "There's someone I want you to meet. I think she can help you."

Help me? With death on her face like that, with those big, staring eyes? How could she possibly help me! I found out later why her eyes had widened. When her friend who had died of cancer entered her house for the first time, he had embraced her, even as I had shaken her hand, and then walked over just as I had done and plopped down wearily in the same spot. It was like a rerun of the same event, only this time in color. And not cancer but clandestinity was consuming me.

"I know someone who will help you," Fanchon said. "Do you want me to talk to him about your problem?"

"Who is it?" I asked.

"Giscard d'Estaing."

"Giscard d'Estaing!?"

I didn't turn white with fear, but I scrambled to my feet, torn by the impulse to run out the door and head for the frontier. Why had Martine brought me here, set me up like this? I pleaded with Fanchon to forget it, and to please not mention my name to that man.

"Okay," she said. "I won't."

France's President, Georges Pompidou, was dying. The whole world knew that. Valéry Giscard d'Estaing, by all accounts an economic and financial genius, had been France's Minister of Finance and Economy, on and off, mostly on, for the last fifteen years. He was one of three men most likely to succeed Pompidou as President of France, the others being the cocky but shallow Jacques Chaban-Delmas, a formerly powerful and popular premier who had resigned before the storms of tax fraud scandals could catch up with him, and François Mitterrand, candidate of the United Left, architect of the unity of the Socialist and Communist parties behind a common program. Chaban-Delmas was the obstacle between Giscard and the support of the governing parties in a general election pitting one or the other against Mitterrand, who was definitely feeling his political Cheerios.

Tainted by scandal, but even more seriously, possessed of a little hollow, pint-sized voice that hinted of vacuousness within, Chaban-Delmas was no sure thing, either in the run-off for the candidacy of the governing coalition, or in the general election that would determine the issue.

Going against Giscard were his aristocratic lineage and bearing, and the way he seemed to look down his nose at you from the TV screen when, periodically, he stepped forth to explain to the nation why and how inflation worked, and why and how he planned to stop it.

Some time later Martine contacted me through a third party—very few people knew my real identity or where I lived or how to contact me—sending word that Fanchon wanted to see me, that night, at her home. It was hard for me to find the courage to keep the rendezvous. But something in my instinct told me to go. So I went.

Fanchon looked less like an undertaker this time and more like a doctor about to tell me the results of the laboratory's analysis. She took me by the arm and asked me to sit down, guiding me to the cushions on the floor. I sat down heavily again, prepared to hear the worst.

"Remember I asked you if you wanted me to talk to Giscard about normalizing your situation?" Fanchon began.

"Yes," I answered. I also remembered that I had asked her not to do it.

Fanchon continued, "I realized that you were afraid, that you could not trust Giscard, of course, so I said nothing more to you about it. But I knew that I could trust Giscard on a point of honor. I knew that he would not betray me. So I explained your situation to him. I told him that you are a black American leader in trouble with the American government, that you are in Paris illegally with your wife and two children, that your situation is desperate, and I asked him to normalize your situation, to give you papers. And I gave him a copy of your book."

"What did he say?" I asked her, breathlessly.

"He will speak to the Minister of Interior about your problem. He will give me the answer Friday."

"He's going to speak to the Minister of the Interior about me? Tell him that I'm in Paris?"

"But don't worry," Fanchon said, smiling. "He will help you. Giscard will not betray me."

I looked at Fanchon, searching her face. For the first time, I realized how strikingly beautiful she was.

ROLAND DUMAS, a prominent French lawyer, was a leading member of the Socialist Party and a part of François Mitterrand's inner circle. In the outer circles, where I had some friends treading the murky waters of French politics, it was said that if Mitterrand became President, Dumas certainly would become a Minister, perhaps of Justice. As a youth in his native Bordeaux, Dumas had joined the Résistance against the Nazi occupation. During the Algerian War of Independence, he was one of the earliest defenders of Algerians caught in the snares of the Napoleonic Code. Though he had married into a rich family and counted Pablo Picasso amongst his clients, Roland had not lost the common touch. He was one of two prominent lawyers in Paris who could be counted on by political refugees in search of asylum or threatened by expulsion. Jean-Jacques de Falice was the other. I had started out with de Falice and ended up with Dumas for my attorney.

When I first arrived in Paris, the circle of friends in whose hands I placed myself arranged for Kathleen and me to meet Maître de Falice in his office. A short, white-haired man whose cherubic face reflected an inner light, de Falice was the embodiment of French concern for Human Rights. He was also a Protestant, and, as such, a member of a persecuted minority, for France is Roman Catholic to the bone.

Like a priest about to hear a dark wayfaring stranger confess his sins and dreading that they might be more than he could handle, de Falice received Kathleen and me almost apologetically. Our friends had briefed him on the

broad outlines of our problems. As we sketched in the
details, de Falice underwent a gradual change. By the end
of our recital, he resembled judge more than priest. Although he himself was with us, his look pronounced our
case next to hopeless, for reasons having mainly to do with
the upcoming political campaign. His advice was to wait
until that storm had passed.

We were living at this time in a two-room walkup apartment on the Rue St. Jacques, in the heart of the Latin
Quarter. The phone rang one day and Revy * wanted to
know if she and her husband could bring over the vener-
able writer-playwright Jean Genet. Of course they could.
By the time Genet had climbed up the five flights of stairs
to reach our apartment, his legs were almost gone. "Don't
worry," he said in breathless French, "with such stairs
you won't be bothered too much by me!"

Genet had made himself a hero to the Black Panther
Party when, back in 1970, he traveled to the United States
to speak out in support of Bobby Seale during his trial
in New Haven, Connecticut, on murder charges. (Seale was
acquitted.) I had read several of Genet's books, and was
therefore a little intimidated by the prospect of encounter-
ing, face to face, such a formidable intellect. Conversing
through translators would have been easier. The translator
insulates you and slows everything down. You have the
chance to hear everything twice, and if what you've said
comes out too weak, or wrong, or doesn't go over too well,
you have a chance to change or amend it. This works fine
when you have some familiarity with the second language,
as I had with French. With Chinese, Arabic, and other such
distant tongues, I lost this particular advantage. But Genet
knew a little English, and I knew a little French, so we
had a lively conversation, in Franglais, as they call it.

---

* A friend, name changed.

As I explained to Genet why I'd come to Europe, and particularly to France, he began to smile and finally burst out laughing.

"You are a child, a baby!" Genet said.

I had been explaining that in leaving Algeria, I had decided to come out of the Third World and the Communist/Socialist world altogether. I wanted to apply to the Social Affairs Commission of the European Community, in Brussels, for political asylum. Juridically, my petition would be properly directed, but in practical terms, I knew that the Community would not act on my petition. However, I felt that having such a petition pending offered an extra lever in case I got popped somewhere and the United States requested my extradition.

Genet had been smiling, twinkle-eyed, as I ran through that. What made him burst out laughing is what I said about France: "France is one of the few countries in the world irretrievably attached to democracy. During the American Revolution, France granted political asylum to Benjamin Franklin and Thomas Paine. Lafayette fought for American freedom. Alexis de Tocqueville wrote a great book explaining America to the world, and to Americans themselves. In our own time, de Gaulle kicked NATO out of France and recognized Communist China. I believe that Europe—and particularly France—is on a collision course with the United States. Given that history, and the present world situation, I believe that there is room in France for me. So here I am."

"It was under the Empire that France gave asylum to the Americans," Genet said, laughing. "I'm afraid you've come along about three hundred years too late!" Genet had on his face an expression of astonishment, as though he couldn't believe all this was happening, or at any rate that I was serious.

As I tried to defend my reasons for coming to France,

I said some positive things about France. This absolutely pushed Genet's button.

"Not only are you a child," Genet said, "you're white!" Then he launched into a violent denunciation of France, historically and currently. He piled up the bodies, the atrocities, the cruel injustices, committed by the French against people of the Third World. By the time he finished, I was somewhat shaken. How could I have made such a mistake? There was no denying that what Genet said was true. Yet I felt that there was something blind and indiscriminate about his total condemnation of the white race and total absolution of people of color. I had just left Algeria, disillusioned, angry at the Third World in general, and in no mood to hear them praised. Yet this conversation had taken me completely by surprise. I had not anticipated it. I had wanted Genet's help and advice, but here I was on the verge of arguing with him. After I got to know Genet better, I was convinced that he would have helped me in any case; we had too much in common and supported too many of the same causes not to have a certain bond between us.

One night not long after this, Genet introduced me to Roland Dumas at the home of one of his friends. "De Falice is a wonderful man, a great lawyer," Genet had said. "He's even a greater human spirit. But your case is too hot politically for him. Only Roland Dumas can deal with your case."

At this meeting, Genet extracted a solemn promise from Dumas, his word of honor, that no matter what happened he would never let me drop. *"Jamais relâcher* Eldridge, *jusqu'au bout,"* Genet made him promise.

"Jamais," Roland Dumas promised, looking from Genet to me. *"Jusqu'au bout."*

Dumas prepared a petition, addressed to Premier Pierre Mesmer as head of government, explaining that I was a fighter for the rights of black Americans against racism and discrimination, and requesting that I be granted political asylum in France and allowed to settle in France with my wife and two children, to live in peace and security. At no point in the text did it state that I was already actually in France. Along with the formal petition for political asylum, Roland Dumas sent an appeal to the government, signed by many outstanding French personalities, including Jean-Paul Sartre and Simone de Bouvoir, and by all the political parties of the Left, except the French Communist Party. The French Communist Party refused to sign, they said, on the advice of the American Communist Party, which was angry with me because I had dared to criticize Angela Davis. The documents were filed.

About two weeks later, since the government had not responded to my petition, François Mitterrand, in his capacity as leader of the opposition in the National Assembly, addressed a question to the government as to why it had not responded to such an urgent request and what did it intend to do.

In time, Raymond Marcellin, the Minister of the Interior, responded for the government. Eldridge Cleaver has been granted political asylum in Algeria. He's doing fine in Algeria. So let him stay in Algeria.

Roland Dumas appealed the government's decision to an appropriate authority, and there the matter rested. He believed that Marcellin already knew that I was in Paris but had decided to avoid the whole issue—for the time being.

WHEN FANCHON told me that she'd already talked to Giscard d'Estaing about my situation, my first impulse was to contact Roland Dumas and tell him everything. But there wasn't that much to tell: a wild-eyed girl, to whom men with terminal illnesses were evidently attracted, said that she'd talked to the Minister of Finance and Economy about my case, and he had promised to take it up with the Minister of the Interior. I didn't want to take a story like that to Dumas. Better to wait for the situation to jell.

The next time I saw Fanchon, she told me the matter was settled and that Giscard had invited Kathleen and me to meet with them for breakfast, at her house, that coming Sunday morning, when he'd explain everything to us. I decided it was time for me to explain everything to Roland Dumas.

Dumas invited Kathleen and me over to his apartment on the Quai de Bourbon, and I told him the story from beginning to end. The question was whether I should show up at that breakfast. For Kathleen, it raised no serious problem. Since she had a valid American passport, she could enter and exit France at will, and could stay for up to six months each time with no visa or permit necessary. But if it was a trap, the police could take me directly to the Spanish or Belgian border and kick me over, into the waiting arms of the FBI.

"On the other hand," Dumas said, "it could very well be on the level. Giscard is a serious man of some integrity. If he's truly involved, as you say, then I think it may be okay. If, however, he's not involved, if the girl is lying, and someone else altogether is behind her, it could be a very touchy situation."

Dumas was leaving Paris for the weekend, taking his children skiing in the Alps. He gave us the phone number of the lodge where he'd be staying. If all went well, I was to call him immediately after breakfast. If an emergency arose, Kathleen was to call him immediately. Meanwhile, we'd hope for the best.

Fanchon instructed me to arrive at her house precisely at 9:00 A.M., not a minute earlier and definitely not a minute later. We arranged to meet Martine at the Zhyer, a cafe at Alesia, a couple minutes walk from Fanchon's atelier. Martine would take Maceo and Joju to an apartment of a friend who lived nearby but who was not in on what was happening. Before splitting up after breakfast, Fanchon would telephone Martine and have her bring them over, because Giscard wanted to meet them.

Sunday morning, we all were up early. Maceo and Joju, a little bit dazed, shared our excitement, although they couldn't understand what was going on.

"Who is Giscard?" Joju kept asking.

"A big Frenchman," I told her.

"Bigger than you?"

"No, he's not bigger than me," I told her. "But he has power. He's going to fix it so you and Ceo can go to school."

When we arrived at the Zhyer, Martine was already there with her son, Stephen. We had time for a *petit café*. I had taken the precaution of having a couple of friends stake out Fanchon's house earlier that morning. I also gave them Dumas's phone number in the mountains. If I was arrested, their immediate task was to assemble a crowd and create such a noise that the police would not spirit me away to the frontier. If anything suspicious happened around Fanchon's house, they were to come to the Zhyer before 8:45, because at that time, Kathleen and I would start walking up Avenue Jean Moulin, toward Fanchon's.

Evidently nothing untoward was up, because no one came. Kathleen and I started walking. It was just the opposite of walking the last mile. Rather than marking the end of everything, this walk was a new beginning. We measured our steps. At precisely 9:00, I rang Fanchon's doorbell.

"*Entrez!*" Fanchon's voice commanded from within.

A tall man wearing khaki-green dungarees, white shirt, and dark green sweater stood near the table with his back toward the door. He was thumbing through a large photo book. Fanchon was nowhere to be seen, but the commotion in the kitchen was eloquent testimony as to her presence. We walked in and stood behind the man.

It was an awkward moment. Although he was obviously aware that we had entered the room, the tall man ignored us for a moment, as though intensely absorbed in the photo book. That was what I call the telltale moment, an employ of time which important people make just to let you know who is in control. After it was established that he controlled time, that we were waiting for him, the tall man turned, sweeping us with his eyes and then looking directly into mine. It was indeed Valéry Giscard d'Estaing. Fanchon chose that moment, as though on cue, to run out of the kitchen in such a way as to dispense with all formality. With a pot of coffee in one hand and a plate of croissants in the other, she immediately provoked everyone into helping her by almost spilling the whole load. She was in control now.

"Permit me to introduce you," Fanchon said, recovering from the near debacle. "*Monsieur Valéry Giscard d'Estaing. Monsieur Eldridge Cleaver et son femme, Kathleen.*"

"I am pleased to meet you," Giscard said in very good English, extending his hand.

We were pleased to meet him and told him so as we shook his hand. I breathed a sigh of relief. So it was all true after all. From the look on Fanchon's face, I could tell that she felt vindicated.

"*À table! À table!*" Fanchon said, startling everybody. She appointed everybody their seat. I sat facing Giscard across the table and Kathleen sat next to Giscard facing Fanchon, who sat next to me.

In France, one of the responsibilities of the Minister of the Interior is organizing and supervising elections. He must guarantee that everything happens in an orderly, legal, and democratic manner. He must keep the results of the balloting above reproach. As a sign that President Georges Pompidou was indeed dying, and also an indication of the direction in which the political winds were blowing, Premier Pierre Mesmer had reshuffled his cabinet. Raymond Marcellin, the dreaded but clumsy super cop, was shifted out of the Ministry of the Interior into Agriculture. He was replaced by Pompidou's protégé, Jacques Chirac, who reminded me of a double-edged razor blade. It was to Chirac that Giscard had talked about my case.

"I told him," Giscard said laughingly, "I would like for him to normalize the situation of my friend, Monsieur Eldridge Cleaver, and his wife. Give them documents permitting them to reside legally in France."

Chirac had noted our names, promising to look into it. A couple of days later, Chirac had come to Giscard with a puzzled look on his face.

"Is there some mistake?" he asked Giscard, spreading my dossier before him. "Are you sure this man is your friend?"

Giscard had thumbed through my file, remarking that it

was quite thick for a man who had never officially been on French territory, had never had a run-in with the French authorities. I was *interdit* in France. I was to be expelled immediately if ever caught on French territory. I was classified as a dangerous terrorist associated with airplane hijacking.

" 'It's nothing,' I told Chirac," Giscard said, laughing as he described the baffled look that came over Chirac's face. But when the Minister of the Interior was sure that there was no mixup, that the man in the dossier and his friend were one and the same, that was the end of it. The matter was closed. It would be taken care of.

"Tuesday night," Giscard said, "I invite you to have dinner with me at my apartment. At that time, I will have detailed instructions for you from the Minister of the Interior."

At the right moment, Fanchon called Martine on the phone and told her to bring the children. They were there in a matter of minutes, as though on cue, providing a perfect reason for abandoning the uncomfortable vis-à-vis of the breakfast table.

Because we had given this moment such a buildup, it was predictable that Maceo and Joju would try to spoil it, first, by refusing to shake hands with Giscard; second, by sulking and carrying on something terrible. They liked people who gave them gifts; toys and candy are what they understood. Giscard was giving them—all four of us—the priceless gift of a new start, a new life, free, more or less, from constantly looking over my shoulder. He also gave Kathleen a beautiful red rose in a little red pot.

THE MINISTRY of Finance and Economy is located in the Louvre, which is now France's greatest museum but once was the palace of its kings. The Louvre houses the world's largest art collection and is the most valuable site in France. It is France's principal tourist attraction, tourism being one of France's major sources of income. Not only did the Minister of Finance and Economy have his office in the Louvre, he also had an apartment there, which has to be the heaviest pad in Paris. It was there that Fanchon took Kathleen and me to dinner.

We arrived punctually at eight o'clock. The security guards were expecting us and waved us toward the elevator. Fanchon pressed a button and the elevator let us out on an upper floor. After visiting China and seeing the palaces of the emperors and empresses, after seeing and touching their delicate, refined, highly artistic furnishings, I've found it difficult to be truly impressed by grandeur on a smaller scale. In fact, it was somehow soothing to my ego to recognize the aesthetic and artistic superiority of the Chinese over Western whites. Western culture and civilization was forever deflated in my eyes.

Yet, as we made our way through an endless series of sumptuous rooms, realizing that this was both a museum and the apartment of my benefactor, I was impressed. I was plunged into confusion precisely because I was unable to separate my feelings, to distinguish the happiness I felt over the occasion, the situation, from the physical locale in which it was all taking place. Those warm, velvety rooms, with their high ceilings, rich colors, crystal chande-

liers, plush carpets and drapes, with everything trimmed
in gold, made a profound and lasting impression upon
me.

We finally found Giscard in an inner chamber. The first
thing I noticed was my book, *Soul On Ice*, in the French
translation, lying on a table next to a comfortable chair.
After greeting and seating us, Giscard resumed that chair.

Small talk, and dinner in another room, passed quickly.
I could have done without dinner, I was so uptight. All I
remember was the surprising white gloves worn by the
waiter to handle the hot dishes and the white paper
wrapped around the bones at the tip of the pork chops, for
handling them without soiling one's hands. After dinner
we retired to the sitting room.

Giscard explained that Kathleen and I had an appointment the next morning with the Prefect of Police. He gave
us an appointment card. To simplify matters, Giscard
would send his personal chauffeur to drive us to the Prefecture, across the street from the Palais de Justice, on the
Ile Saint-Louis. We agreed to meet his chauffeur at Fanchon's house the next morning, and return to Giscard's
museum apartment the day after that, to celebrate, at the
same hour.

Everything went off smoothly, without a hitch, but not
without a twitch. My body chemistry had gone crazy.
Giscard's chauffeur was driving a big black official DS, and
he had a small tricolored disc which he flashed on the
guards at the entrance to the Prefecture, snapping them
to attention and allowing us to drive into the courtyard.
The Prefecture of Paris lies between the Place Saint-Michel
and the Place du Châtelet. During the year in which I lived
clandestinely in Paris, I had passed it many times, in taxis
and in private cars. But always with a sinking feeling, with
a feeling of dread, knowing that if I ever got popped I'd
end up there some day, in chains. To enter, escorted by

the Minister's chauffeur and friend, had not occurred to me as a possibility. Even when I had sat in the cafes at Châtelet, looking out over the Seine at that very Prefecture, wishing that I had legal status, I had never dreamed, in my wildest moment, that it could happen, and like this!

Monsieur le préfet had received orders from the Minister of the Interior to normalize our situation, and we had arrived in the car of the Minister of Finance. There was no question but that *Monsieur le préfet* was going to comply with the order. But he had not been given an explanation, and he'd like to understand. If neither Giscard nor Chirac had given an explanation to the prefect, I thought it best that I didn't either, so when the prefect pressed me on the point, I suggested that he take the matter up with Chirac or Giscard. Not understanding exactly what he was dealing with, *Monsieur le préfet* beat a hasty retreat.

"No, no," he said, "it's not necessary. I understand that some things are TOP SECRET."

The prefect had been speaking in French, but he said "top secret" in English, the way the French say Chicago (as the symbol of a wicked city), or hot dog, or drug store. He then asked me how long I had been in France.

"One year," I told him in French.

He looked confused, as though he had not understood, could not believe his ears. So he asked me again. Again I said one year. Having said that, I felt that I had said too much, because *Monsieur le préfet* was seething. He didn't like all this one bit. It must have been unprecedented in his experience. It reminded him, he said, of World War II, of the Nazi occupation, of his own participation in the Résistance, and his experience with living clandestinely, of making and using false identity documents.

"We French have been through it all," *Monsieur le préfet* said. "We understand."

Kathleen and I signed the forms laid out on the prefect's

desk, and in a moment we were in possession of the magic papers allowing us to remain in France as long as we liked. We thanked *Monsieur le préfet* and rushed out to Giscard's car to show our papers to Fanchon and the chauffeur.

We had our celebration with Giscard in his museum apartment. He gave Kathleen a Sikh bracelet and me a word of advice.

"President Pompidou will soon die," Giscard said. "I shall become the next President of France. At that time you will have no problem. In the meantime, we must be careful. For the moment it's better if your new situation remains quiet. There is Michel Jobert, our Minister of Foreign Affairs, to consider. If the Americans learn of your new status, they will take it up with Jobert. Nothing could come of it, of course. You are perfectly safe. We just prefer not to be obliged to explain anything to M. Jobert. But above all else, you are free to remain on the territory of the Republic of France for as long as you like."

We drank a toast, to our new freedom, and to the next President of France.

THROUGH LAWYERS in the United States, I had sent out feelers about the conditions on my return, what I could expect should this develop. The Nixon administration was satisfied to let me "twist slowly in the wind" of Southern France.

I discovered that the split which had developed within the Panther organization had left me on the losing side. People that I had trusted to be my advocate in America ended up sabotaging my case. Representative Ron Dellums, an old Bay Area acquaintance, concluded that there was no place for me in the United States. I was becoming more and more depressed by this European isolation. Here I was, camping in France, trying to write, attempting to support a wife and two youngsters, and emotionally defeated by causes, banners, and slogans which no longer worked and were increasingly fraudulent.

I suppose I could have chronicled the end of the revolutionary movements that had enticed me: The Black Panthers were in a level of aging disintegration. Eastern and Western branches in the United States had gone through their own pitched battles for supremacy. Stokely had said goodbye. David Hilliard, our former office manager in Oakland, was sounding like the Secretary of State. I was read out of the Party for being too militant and too dangerous. Fortunately, wars change politics, and the wars in America were coming to a close. In my despair some flickers of hope were appearing.

I might have written about the god that failed—or even that Mao that failed. For communism had nothing to offer me but another chapter in tyranny. I had been trying to escape that all my life and ended up running headlong into its main centers. My own experience as a parent was basic enough philosophy to instruct me that there was a Supreme Being, with or without Karl Marx's endorsement. My convictions jelled so that I was willing to acknowledge that there was a God who had designed and ruled over this universe, much to the chagrin of my French revolutionary drinking friends. When they choked on that, I announced that their whole business, industrial, and technological scene was absolutely trash. Eternally, they lifted a glass to the Eiffel Tower, and I replied that it was America which built the electric typewriters, and until they had something like IBM, they had better stick with busts of Napoleon. I was getting sarcastic and cynical: sarcastic about the minor league gloating of the Europeans, and cynical about my own attempts to create a meaningful philosophy of life. I was having a difficult time with the latter, particularly when observing the development of my youngsters in France.

Some of my friends announced that they were going deeper into the Third World. I forgave them, but how could they ignore all the warning signs that lurked beneath the glowing rhetoric of peace and freedom and liberation jargon? Behind their preachments and grand declarations of freedom and justice, I could smell the rot and hear the gunfire. I had just enough of that from age fourteen. So here I was in France believing that if Benjamin Franklin could gain from the experience, then maybe Eldridge Cleaver would share some of the same benefits two hundred years later.

But I had my children in French schools, picking their way through European culture. Not good. First, their language changed. It was a struggle to keep English number one around the house. Then my son started talking and playing soccer. I was dismayed to think that he would not ever play football and know the excitement and challenge of the premier American sport. I looked around at other exiles and saw that they were slowly being bent into the French mold. I felt doomed.

I seemed to pivot, mentally and emotionally, between absolute despair and temporary hope. As the American scene improved and the wretched climate of the Sixties faded into the possible Seventies, I revived my American dreams of returning. Suddenly Nixon was forced out of office. Ford seemed to be a reasonable type. Lo and behold, John Mitchell, who had signed my last warrant, was heading for prison himself. The FBI was being turned inside out.

Not only were the Nixons and Agnews out of office, many of my old friends were getting elected and gaining nice appointments. Friends were getting elected to Congress; another became lieutenant governor of California; some were now mayors of cities that were once in flames. Talk about a brave new world; it looked as if it was on its way. Perhaps, just maybe, this was the right time to go home. Sure, fly home. So I contacted these old friends and said, "Hey, remember me? How about helping me get back home?" Surely, if the astronauts can come back from the moon, I could stroll through California again.

"Well, no, not really, Eldridge. We don't want any trouble," they said. I had forgotten that they were now Establishment Blacks, full of black awareness and black power and black is beautiful and all that, but they honestly would not help this fugitive Negro. Anyway, what would Huey Newton think? I didn't care what Huey Newton thought. Very soon, Huey Newton got indicted on some brand new charges, and ran away to Cuba. So I recontacted my old friends.

Negative, negative, they all said and wrote and sighed.

One good buddy flew over from the States and told me face to face to forget it. There was no help, no assistance, no interest in Brother Cleaver. The political and social blacks have no space for the Cleavers. Everything was changed. The black people in charge don't want to hear your name, Eldridge. There is no place for you, so why don't you just settle down and become a black Frenchman and enjoy all those French pastries. It was like a sentence —another era of serving time.

That was like a thread I was suspended from being cut. I began to experience a severe depression. Perhaps I have been crazy all my life, but I never went around depressed or brooding or tormented or anything like that. In this situation in France, I began to be terribly depressed. I began to feel completely, totally useless, burdened. I began to put a lot of pressure on my wife with the idea of driving her away and forcing her to go back to the United States and take the children. I was the obstacle. Kathleen had never been arrested in her life. My children had never been arrested. They were free. I was the fugitive and it was my fault we were locked out; and I began to feel guilty to the extent that I could hardly face them. To be around them I felt miserable, guilty, seeing the emptiness that had become our life.

In addition to our house in Paris, we had an apartment on the Mediterranean coast near Cannes and Nice. Here I had all of my books and filing cabinets, typewriter, manuscripts; and I could go there to be alone to write. I would go there and just sit and stare out in space with a blank mind—just miserable—becoming more and more miserable as if there were no end to misery—just becoming worse and worse and worse. I would return to Paris, and that didn't help. I'd go back down to the coast, and that didn't help. I was running back and forth—getting worse and worse.

Finally, one night in Paris I became aware of the hopelessness of our situation. We were sitting down to dinner and we had two candles on the table. All the lights in the house were out, and I was suddenly struck that this was a perfect metaphor for our life: our life was empty—there was no light in our life. We were going through an empty ritual, eating in the same spirit in which you might drive to a gas station and fill up the tank. It was meaningless, pointless, getting nowhere.

I returned to the Mediterranean Coast and began thinking of putting an end to it all by committing suicide. I really began to think about that. I was sitting up on my balcony, one night, on the thirteenth floor—just sitting there. It was a beautiful Mediterranean night—sky, stars, moon hanging there in a sable void. I was brooding, downcast, at the end of my rope. I looked up at the moon and saw certain shadows . . . and the shadows became a man in the moon, and I saw a profile of myself (a profile that we had used on posters for the Black Panther Party—something I had seen a thousand times). I was already upset and this scared me. When I saw that image, I started trembling. It was a shaking that came from deep inside, and it had a threat about it that this mood was getting worse, that I could possibly disintegrate on the scene and fall apart. As I stared at this image, it changed, and I saw my former heroes paraded before my eyes. Here were Fidel Castro, Mao Tse-tung, Karl Marx, Frederick Engels, passing in review—each one appearing for a moment of time, and then dropping out of sight, like fallen heroes. Finally, at the end of the procession, in dazzling, shimmering light, the image of Jesus Christ appeared. That was the last straw.

I just crumbled and started crying. I fell to my knees, grabbing hold of the banister; and in the midst of this shaking and crying the Lord's Prayer and the 23rd Psalm came into my mind. I hadn't thought about these prayers for years. I started repeating them, and after a time I gained some control over the trembling and crying. Then I jumped up and ran to my bookshelf and got the Bible. It was the family Bible my mother had given to me because I am the oldest boy—the oldest son. And this Bible . . . when Kathleen left the United States, she brought with her a very small bag, and instead of grabbing the Communist Manifesto or *Das Kapital*, she packed that Bible. That is the Bible that I grabbed from the shelf that night and in which I turned to the 23rd Psalm. I discovered that my memory really had not served me that well. I got lost somewhere between the Valley of the Shadow of Death and the overflowing cup. But it was the Bible in which I searched and found that psalm. I read through it. At that time I didn't even know where to find the Lord's Prayer. I looked for it desperately. Pretty soon the type started swimming before my eyes, and I lay down on the bed and went to sleep.

That night I slept the most peaceful sleep I have ever known in my life. I woke up the next morning with a start, as though someone had touched me, and I could see in my mind the way, all the way back home, just as clear as I've ever seen anything. I saw a path of light that ran through a prison cell. . . . This prison cell was a dark spot on this path of light, and the meaning, which was absolutely clear to me, was that I didn't have to wait on any politician to help me get back home. I had it within my power to get back home by taking that first step, by surrendering; and it was a certainty that everything was going to be all right. I just knew that—that was the solution, and I would be all right if I would take that step.

WHEN GOD PUTS HIS hand upon a life all things are made new. But that renewal is an unfolding process. My life was changed forever that night on the balcony beneath the moonlit, star-spangled Mediterranean sky. But more change, much more, was yet to come, and as I write this, I know that still more change lies ahead as each day has been a new revelation. Each day teaches me anew the marvel and joy and fulfillment flowing from awareness of the presence of God through his Holy Spirit within and around me.

My faith, belief, and comfort have all grown to such an extent that when I look back to the day I decided to surrender, I marvel that I made it. I know now better than anyone else how dependent upon God I was. My spiritual legs were so weak I could hardly stand on them, but I knew that God was present and that he knew about me because he had reached out and touched me and turned me around. He had shown me the way out of the dead-end of my choices. In a real sense I became sort of a spectator, waiting anxiously to see what God would do next.

What he had already done was to take all the fear out of my life—most of all of police, prison, and courts. I no longer had one iota of fear about what would happen if I surrendered. In place of the former fear, God had given me an enthusiasm, an eagerness and an assurance that I would come through whatever ordeal issued from my surrender. What more could I need?

I felt so greatly relieved, and at the same time, astounded. Kathleen also. An excitement entered our life.

We were taking a new initiative: out of stagnation unto death, a fresh spark of life; out of hopelessness, boundless hope—with assurance that that hope would be fulfilled.

Next to be astounded were my lawyers in Paris at the firm of Samuel Pisar. I went first to Carl Salans, to whom I had been assigned by the head of the firm, and asked them to contact the American government and organize my surrender.

In Salans's face I could see shock, disbelief, then signs of strong emotional upheaval. But almost immediately he had himself under control and was organizing a meeting with Samuel Pisar himself. (Pisar, a man of powerful intellect and profound spiritual anointing, was the youngest survivor of Auschwitz and had narrowly escaped execution along with his mother and brothers and sisters. Thirty years later, accompanied by the President of France, he returned to stand upon the very same spot from which he had last seen his mother. Samuel Pisar is a blazing flame.) After satisfying himself that I was in as sound mind as ever, that I was aware of what I was doing, Pisar gave the word to go ahead.

The American authorities, however, when informed of my desire to surrender, were very suspicious. They figured I was up to something, that I had some sort of dark scheme up my sleeve. Finally they concluded that I was trying to get my hands on a passport. I thought this was ridiculous because I had access to all the passports I would ever need. Someone came up with the idea of giving me a letter in lieu of a passport. I said, "Great, I'll take it!"

But even with the question of the travel document solved, a lot of red tape, both American and French, had to be waded through. I was told that Judge Harold Tyler, the number two man in the Justice Department under Attorney General Levy, had taken personal charge of organizing my surrender. From the moment I entered American custody to my final destination in the Federal Prison in San Diego, California, at least half a dozen bureaucracies had to be coordinated, including the Justice Department, the Federal Bureau of Prisons, TWA, the California Department of Corrections, the offices of the Alameda County District Attorney and the California Attorney General.

The French government viewed my request with equal suspicion, not to mention astonishment. I had to sign a declaration absolving them of all responsibility. They wanted to make sure I was not surrendering because of any pressure being put upon me. They wanted to know if the CIA was bothering me and whether I was being threatened in any way. When I assured them that everything was on the up and up, that I was surrendering of my own volition, they wished me good luck, their astonishment still showing.

It took about three weeks for Judge Tyler to get the whole package together. Those three weeks were among the most nerve-racking in my life. I went through precisely the same agonizing countdown I had gone through many times before—that ticking off of the minutes, scratching off of the days, which a prisoner goes through just before the end of his sentence. In those final hours madness beats upon your door. You worry that something might go wrong to upset the applecart. You wish that time would speed up but it seems to be slowing down.

A few times I woke up at night in the middle of a bad dream. For twenty years I had had more or less the same bad dream every night (I thank God through his son Jesus Christ for setting me free of that nightmare!). In that dream, I was always in a desperate situation, either in prison or outside in the free world, but just on the verge of getting arrested. It was like being sucked down into a pit each night, and for this reason my sleep was without rest; there was no peace in my repose. While I was waiting for Judge Tyler, I started having a dream each night of waking up in the wee hours of the morning, rushing to the bars on the front of the cell and grabbing hold of them, giving them a futile shake. In this new dream, I would always be suffocating and fighting for air to breathe. It was like looking ahead at what lay in wait for me, at what it would be like once I got in prison and I needed to breathe a breath of fresh air. What would happen then when I woke up and shook the bars and found they were real and not the stuff of dreams?

The day finally came that Judge Tyler gave the go-ahead. The first thing Kathleen and I did was to send our children, Maceo and Joju, back to the United States, to my mother's house in Pasadena, California. This act was laden with meaning for us. During the years of our exile, we often saw storms brewing on the horizon, and we could not always be sure what lay beyond the storm. At such times we always sent Maceo and Joju to a safe nesting place with people who loved and cared for them, people who could be counted on just in case. But this time when we sent our children home, we knew we were sending them where our hearts were, where we were going.

Next I was to leave. Kathleen would bring up the rear, waiting behind in Paris for me to come down for a soft landing. Then, after closing down our house in Paris, she would fly back home herself.

Many people have looked at what happened and concluded that I must have made a deal with the authorities. This is very intriguing to me: what they are saying is that such things just do not happen, that the whole surrender event was extraordinary and therefore a pay-off was involved. They have to insist on this—otherwise they would have to consider the miracle of salvation involved.

Yes. They are right. I did make a deal; I made a deal with Jesus Christ! Yes, as well as I was able to understand it at that moment, I sold out; I sold out to Jesus! When I surrendered, I was stumbling ahead on faith and a vision, on assurance of the reality and truth of God, but I was still stumbling.

Little did I realize how totally I was surrendering. Nor did I understand that I was surrendering on two levels—to the civil authorities and to God. I am harping on this point, screaming out what seems to me a very vital fact—the act of stepping out on faith—because I clearly did not know what was going to happen. All I had was the assurance that things were going to turn out all right.

But even that assurance was going to be tested in time. The only guarantee I received through my lawyers from the Justice Department was that my security was guaranteed against the California Department of Correction, the Oakland Police Department, and other state and local agencies. Later on I was to regret that the agreement had not also stipulated the name of the Alameda County Sheriff's Department, into whose hands I ultimately fell.

So one day in 1975, Kathleen and I visited the American Embassy in Paris, accompanied by Attorney Salans, to fill out an application for a passport. The embassy functionary, obviously uptight, asked me to raise my right hand and swear, repeating after him, that the information I had put into the application was true and correct. The moment of truth had arrived.

Then in November the day came that we went to the airport in Paris. I was about a half an hour late through the heavy traffic, but I was there in plenty of time to catch the plane. I had been told that two gentlemen would meet me at the airport and would accompany me back to New York. Technically they had the power to place me under arrest once the plane took off from French soil, but I would not be arrested until I disembarked from the plane at Kennedy Airport in New York.

The two men who met me at the airport in Paris showed me FBI credentials. One man was black and one was white. With one in front and one behind me, we boarded the big TWA 747. Tension developed steadily when we had to remain on board on the ground for about an hour because of a problem unrelated to our plane. Finally we took off, and after the lights behind the no-smoking and fasten-seat-belt signs went out, everybody relaxed.

It was strange to see who was in the first-class section that day—a prisoner, the FBI and journalists, lots of them. They had been in Paris covering the visit of President Ford to French President Giscard d'Estaing. One of them, Tom Jarriel, was especially interesting to me since I had seen him on TV many times. Sitting in the nose cone of that 747 and listening to Tom Jarriel gave me the sensation that I was looking at a live TV newscast.

When the plane landed in New York, a warrant for my arrest was read to me as soon as my feet hit the ground. I was placed under arrest, my hands forced behind my back and handcuffed there. My heart started racing as the FBI agents grabbed me by each arm and led me through a door into a room filled with journalists. Flashbulbs and cameras blinking and flashing, they tossed hundreds of questions at me simultaneously while stampeding and trampling upon each other. The agents plowed a path through the center of the journalists, using me as the plow. I thought I was going to get trampled—what I hated about handcuffs was how vulnerable they make you to any outside force; I kept thinking of how Lee Harvey Oswald got assassinated while wearing them—but we finally reached the FBI station at the airport where I was finger-printed and photographed.

At one point we entered a section of the building into which the agents were evidently not allowed to take their personal firearms. They all pulled out their guns and gave them to one man—and to my amazement there were just too many guns for him to handle. It was an eerie feeling. Flashing back on every country of my experience, I could remember nothing like this. For the first time in my life, I could see how really absurdly overarmed America is, how totally reliant upon guns we are. How different it can be in this world!

After being booked by the FBI, I was taken directly before a U.S. commissioner to be arraigned on the fugitive warrant. Inside the commissioner's courtroom, the FBI agents took the handcuffs off me. I felt completely wiped out by the experience of the handcuffs. The commissioner, the U.S. attorney, and some attorneys who appeared for me by previous arrangement, argued about whether or not I was going to resist extradition to California—a process that could take many months if one wanted to drag it out. They were also arguing over the amount at which my bail should be set. When I ran away back in 1968, my bail had been $50,000.00. I was interested in having it remain as low as possible—at $50,000.00, I hoped—but the U.S. attorney wanted to raise it to $100,000.00. Finally, it was agreed that if I did not resist extradition to California, then they would not raise my bail, leaving that to the California authorities.

I asked then why it was necessary for me to be handcuffed. I had traveled thousands of miles to surrender, so why was I now going to run away? I had come back home to put an end to my running. I was not going to run again. The answer was that that is what the book calls for. I asked for a stipulation that I not be handcuffed during the plane ride from New York to San Diego. The federal marshals denied my request, refusing to transport me unless I was handcuffed.

Judge Tyler solved the problem by arranging for guards from the Federal Bureau of Prisons to transport me to

California without any handcuffs. I appreciated this gesture, for I had been free too long. Every fiber in my body was crying out against restraint, and I needed time to make the psychological adjustment. Thanks to Judge Tyler, I arrived in San Diego ready for prison.

Returning to the United States after almost eight years abroad was bound to be something of a cultural shock. But having to deal with cultural shock at the same time as with the shock of going to prison is heavier than a double whammy. But there was no shock.

There was only one shock in my life and that was what God was doing. He was taking me someplace; one thing was leading to another. What was he going to do with me? Where was I going? It wasn't my plan—it was his plan, now unfolding in my life. I was awestruck. I was calm, I was cool, I was collected. I had nothing to hide, nothing to conceal, nothing to defend, and I felt free. And every step of the way I felt free. I was not in prison, and I knew what it meant to be in prison. Something else was going on. I was passing through prison; I was in prison but not in prison.

I was taken to the Metropolitan Correctional Center in San Diego. Something very important happened to me in that jail, something that at the time struck me as a negative event. There was in San Diego a young man who was the assistant minister in a church. His name was George Stevens. George had been a black militant, closely involved with the Black Panther Party and other organizations during the sixties. George found Jesus Christ and became a minister. He asked the warden for permission to visit me. The warden okayed the visit provided that I agreed.

I was very happy for the chance to talk to someone, so George Stevens came in one day, wearing a Stetson hat and carrying a Bible in one hand. I got ready for a boring conversation. George said that there was something going on in my life and that the Lord had put a burden upon him to come to visit me. Never before have I been visited by such a man. It was a strange meeting. I poured out to him what was on my heart. It was new to me but I was in the midst of the first blushes of coming clean.

I was coming clean with everybody, it seems, even though I think the FBI agents who came to question me felt I was holding back on them. But in fact I talked with them with the same enthusiasm and with the same purgative effect upon my soul as when I talked with anybody else, except that I refused to give them information about other people. I rendered to Caesar only what belonged to him, preserving for God what is his. (I think the FBI has some role confusion on this point.)

So I talked to George Stevens about the spiritual sparks going off in my life. At a certain point, George said, "Eldridge, I'm going to do something, can I?" I asked him what he was going to do. I told him that he was responsible for whatever he did. George took the Bible and held it up before my face. "Eldridge Cleaver, this is Jesus Christ," George said. "Jesus Christ, this is Eldridge Cleaver."

It was a baffling moment. My immediate reaction was to get angry with George as though he had played a game with me. I felt as though he was putting me down or something. George noticed my reaction and pretty soon we ended the conversation and he went out of the jail, but he left me transfixed with that introduction. I brooded over it; I began to read the Bible regularly; I began to think more about God; I began to read about Jesus Christ and to really think on a profound level about him.

On January 2, 1976, I was taken to the Alameda County Jail—across the bay from San Francisco—and I remained there for the next eight months. Many people think that I returned to the United States and was released directly to the streets. First of all, I went before a black judge and he raised my bail from $50,000.00 to $100,000.00. Even if I had had the money, which I didn't, I would not have been able to get out on bail because the state prison authorities had a "hold" placed upon me on the grounds that I was a parole violator. The fact is that I was no longer under the jurisdiction of the California Adult Authority, but they had illegally asserted such jurisdiction over me and for this reason I had to remain in jail nine months—the amount of time it took to file a writ of habeas corpus and get it before a judge. When the judge had the hearing, he ordered the Adult Authority to let me go or he would let me go.

During this period of waiting, a few of the deputies of the Alameda County Sheriff's Department were tightening the screws upon me at every opportunity, from stirring up trouble between me and other prisoners to interfering with every procedure relating to me. Members of the Black Panther Party held a series of press conferences denouncing me as an FBI informer and a CIA agent, claiming that I had secretly testified before a session of a Senate Judiciary Committee. To top it off they asked the black people not to help me.

It was very clear to me that this was the moment of truth of my entire life. All of my old friends, with the exception of two or three, rejected me and would not even come down to the county jail to visit me. When Kathleen tried to talk to them about my case, they gave her the cold shoulder. We were isolated.

I felt totally and completely alone. Though Kathleen was with me every step of the way and never faltered, I was alone in another sense that nobody could share with me. I was in jail. I was on the spot. It was I who did jump up in the middle of the night and grab those bars, shaking them and trying to get a breath of fresh air, as I had foreseen in my recurring bad dreams. It was I who was alone in the middle of those long and lonely nights, who had absolutely no other hope, no other place to turn, who had already turned everywhere else in search of health and hope. Now everything else was gone and I turned more and more to God.

But it was also during this nine months of waiting, locked in a jail cell, that I was to experience the clearest and most open activity of God in my life, as he seemed to send the right person at the right time down to the precise moment. He sent Glenn Morrison and the other brother members of the God Squad—a nickname of an organization called Follow-up Ministries which specializes in bringing the gospel to men and women in jail and prison in the state of California.

Glenn was a regular visitor at the Alameda County Jail, and he gave me a Bible on one of his early visits, which I read avidly. But I was still shy about joining in any of the prayer times Glenn had with some of the other prisoners.

When Glenn and the others would form a circle, close their eyes and hold hands and pray, the hostile guys in the tank would throw bars of soap at them or flick water at them with a brush that had been dipped in the commode. You could see the hate in their eyes, and their obscene comments clashed violently with Glenn's soft-spoken prayers. There was no way then that I could bring myself to be a part of that circle—the tough guys would think I had an angle or was a softy. And I wasn't about to turn my back on them or close my eyes; I'd been in too many jails for that.

But in the lonely and quiet night hours I would sit and think about it all. Tears were close to the surface, and at times I would find myself sobbing uncontrollably. I'd taken some first steps in reaching out to God that moonlight night on the Mediterranean coast, but deep inside lurked the haunting feeling that there was something more to it than I had discovered so far.

Then one day in the second week of February, tired of running away, I joined the circle and listened intently to Glenn's talk and his prayer. He stressed the importance of a personal commitment to Jesus Christ—that it wasn't enough just to know that God exists but that complete freedom comes through inviting Christ into our life. I suppose those same words had fallen on my ears before, but this time I really heard them.

The rest of the day I reflected on what I'd heard and felt. I began to see that I had been focusing intellectually on God and Jesus Christ. Instead of praying, I had just been thinking about God. Now for the first time I saw the difference between that and actually talking to God.

Late that night I confronted the reality of my intense need, and my resistance evaporated. I confessed the name of Jesus Christ. I asked him into my life. I asked him to be my personal Savior. I laid all my sins at the foot of his cross and he set me free.

As I began crying tears of joy, God then began unraveling the mess. In my isolation he sent me brand new friends, brothers and sisters in Christ. My mail exploded. My old friends sent me hate letters, condemning me, calling me a traitor and a turncoat, rejecting me. Some expressed hope that I would rot in jail. But this was more than overbalanced by all of the wonderful people who sent me letters of love and encouragement. Those letters nourished the spiritual embryo that had been planted in my heart, and it was what I call the Christian grapevine that sustained me and kept me going in those dark moments.

The Alameda County Sheriff's Department tried by every means to block communication between me and the outside world. They refused to allow me to speak to the press; in fact, they refused as much as possible anything in my regard. While it was perfectly legal for me to make phone calls, I was dependent upon the guards to dial the numbers. But most of them refused to be the least bit cooperative. It seemed that the whole intention was to hide me or to make people forget about me so that I could be more easily shoveled on down and into the state prison. Two guards in particular seemed to get sadistic pleasure from getting to me any way they could. At one point they told me to watch out for poison in my food, that there was a rumor that poison had been smuggled into the jail and that it would be used to get me. Then when my food was brought in, they would snicker over my confusion as to whether I should take a chance in eating it. There seemed to be forces that were trying to drive me deeper and deeper and deeper into the pit and I was very careful as to who came to see me and who wrote to me, very careful not to fall into some kind of trap or to stumble into some kind of setup that would aggravate my situation. It was a desperate moment and I knew that everything was on the line.

It was in this situation that I received my first letter from Arthur De Moss, President of National Liberty Corporation in Valley Forge, Pennsylvania. I had never heard of him before, but he turned out to be God-sent to me in my hour of need. It seems that Art had just happened to read an article by Russell Chandler in the *Los Angeles Times* which described the wave of conversions taking place in many jails as a result of various prison ministries. Russ included something of my story and Art felt impressed to contact me.

This started a series of exchanges. Each of Art's letters brought words of encouragement that were deeply mean-

ingful to me at the time. Frequently the Scripture references he shared penetrated right to the point of my deepest
needs and gave me the will and the strength to go on.

After a time, Art said he wanted to come see me, so arrangements were made through my attorneys and clearance was obtained for his visit. In spite of our exchanges
of letters, I was strongly apprehensive the day I walked
into the attorney's room at the jail to meet Art in person
for the first time. During my months in jail, all sorts of
kooks had been trying to get to me, not to mention the
constant efforts of the FBI to question me, so I had developed an excessively defensive attitude toward anyone
who wanted to see me. But as soon as Art started to talk,
all of my apprehension and suspicion faded away. We
talked and shared with each other for almost two hours,
and during that time I came to know without question that
Art cared for me in the Lord in a very special way.

I have a special warm spot in my heart for all the
brothers and sisters who visited me while I was in jail.
Their visitation kept me going. It made the difference between living and dying, between hope and despair. I really
appreciated the things people sent to me—the letters,
some containing biblical references, and the books and
cards and all kinds of encouragement. A brother named
Ken Overstreet who is head of Youth for Christ in San
Diego was one of those who befriended me, and there were
many members of churches and other religious groups
who visited me. A beloved black bishop came from another state to visit me. He embraced me as dear brother
and prayed for me. I praise the Lord for this shower of
Christian love and for all these wonderful people who
came into my life at that time. I now claim many of them
as my wonderful and beautiful friends as well as brothers
and sisters in Jesus Christ.

A couple of months after Art De Moss's visit, my attorneys were finally able to unravel the legal maze that had prevented my eligibility for bail. While it had been set at $100,000.00, even if the money had been raised, I couldn't have gotten out of jail because of the parole hold on me by the California Prison System dating back to 1968. But when the judge ruled in my favor at the habeas corpus hearing in August of 1976, the State of California dropped its claim against me, and after months in jail without possibility of release, there was now, for the first time, an opportunity for freedom if I could raise bail.

Now, God needed someone to go my bail because I certainly didn't have it, and he needed a gambler. Who else would put up $100,000.00 for Eldridge Cleaver, who had already run away and jumped a $50,000.00 bail eight years before? That is just what the Lord found for me in Art De Moss, a born-again gambler, and I just thank the Lord for sending him to help at that particular time.

But I have come to see that Art wasn't betting on me; he was betting on the Lord and the power of the gospel to change a man. For me, this was the perfect example of someone who was willing to back up personal beliefs with material possessions.

Friday, the 13th of August, 1976, was a day packed with drama and suspense. A representative of Art De Moss was due to arrive at San Francisco International Airport at around 2:00 P.M. with adequate securities to obtain the $100,000 bail. While I've not been overly superstitious about Friday the 13th, I've always been a bit cautious about what happened on that day. But I did have cause to be worried because since we had won the habeas corpus decision, the Alameda County district attorney and the Sheriff's Department were really angry over the possibility of my getting out of jail. I felt sure they and the judge would put any possible obstacle in my path—and they did.

Through a technicality, the judge refused to accept Art's

stock as security. This brought on a flurry of activity on the part of my attorney and Art's representative. But by 4:45 P.M., just fifteen minutes before the 5:00 P.M. deadline, they arrived at the jail with the bond. We had beat the clock. Now all the legalities had been complied with and it was no longer possible for the judge and the jail authorities to stall.

At 5:30 P.M. I went down the elevator—to freedom for the first time in nine months, and into the confusion of a press conference. The reporters had been waiting around all day, and they were not to be denied.

It was a puzzling few minutes for some of the reporters, especially the ex-radicals; I'd known several of them in past years and had talked to them from almost the same spot in my revolutionary Black Panther days. It was a bewildering scenario for them as they attempted to fit together the pieces and come to terms with Eldridge Cleaver the Christian.

The drive across the bay to San Francisco that late afternoon of Friday the 13th stands out vividly in my memory. The sights and sounds and smells as we picked our way through the traffic on the San Francisco Bay Bridge were heady stuff. The sun was slanting brightly across the stairsteps of the San Francisco skyline; the Golden Gate and the distant hills of Marin County were symbolic of the openness and freedom which were now mine—a permanent freedom, I hoped, although for the moment it was impossible to know.

After a brief celebration party at my lawyer's apartment, Kathleen and I spent the weekend at San Francisco's Fairmount Hotel. On Monday we flew to Los Angeles for the reunion with Maceo and Joju, who were staying with my mother and attending Pasadena Christian School. Excitement welled up within me as we sped across Los Angeles and up the arroyo toward Pasadena with its rugged San Gabriel mountains backdrop.

I had seen Maceo and Joju just one time over the past nine months, in the Alameda County Jail. A heavy glass partition separated us, and we had to talk over the telephone—I couldn't even touch them. It was a frightening experience for the children and a heartrending one for me. We decided they shouldn't visit again, so it had been a long time since I'd seen them.

Our reunion in the driveway of my mother's home was everything I had anticipated, and more. I was all but smothered by flailing arms and legs. The children's shouts of joy blanked out everything for several minutes. And then as we walked up to the door, there stood my mother. Tears rolled down her lined cheeks as we embraced. Following my father's death, Mother had especially prayed for my return to America and freedom. And for thirty years she had been praying that I would become a Christian. Now as we looked deeply into each other's eyes, she knew that her prayers had been answered on both counts—no longer was I the "white sheep" of the family.

The press had found me in San Francisco and now they tracked me down in Pasadena, so after a day or two, we sought refuge in San Diego. It was important that we be left alone to give me an opportunity to collect my thoughts and begin to get perspective and a sense of direction. In a very real sense I was suffering from the cultural shock of reentry into the everyday world of free people. Believe me, I was dazzled and bewildered by it all.

It must have been the Lord's special time for us to be in San Diego, because Billy Graham was right in the middle of a crusade there. Since I was keeping in touch with Art De Moss daily by telephone and sharing with him my unfolding activities and whereabouts, Ken Overstreet learned from Art that I was in San Diego. Billy Graham told Ken he wanted to see me but couldn't until the crusade was over; however, I did spend a couple of hours with associate evangelist Leighton Ford in his hotel room. It was a rich time for me as we talked and prayed and I shared my experiences and witness with him.

After the close of the San Diego crusade, arrangements were made for me to visit with Billy Graham in his room at the Marriott Hotel on Century Boulevard near the Los Angeles International Airport. I was tense and nervous as we threaded our way across town to the hotel. Here I was about to meet a man I had actually hated most of my life. Years before I'd had a chance to meet him when he preached at a rally at San Quentin Prison, but I had refused to attend the rally or have anything to do with it or him.

T. W. Wilson met us in the lobby of the Marriott, and my anxiety faded a bit because of his warm and casual manner. But when we got to Billy Graham's room, I was put at ease immediately by Billy's uninhibited embrace and friendly, relaxed manner. The next hour or so was a high time for me as we talked and prayed together. His acceptance of me as a person and Christian brother at that time was precisely the kind of encouragement and affirmation I needed desperately. In looking back now, I realize that the most significant thing for me to come out of that conversation was this one particular bit of advice: "Eldridge," he said, "one thing you must never forget—never embarrass the Lord." That counsel has served me well many times since as I've struggled through lonely moments of decision.

It was during a later visit with Billy Graham that he told me his wife, Ruth, had a picture of me on her wall and had been praying for me for many years. As I've traveled during the two years since then, many others have said the same thing. Somehow now I'm coming to understand just a little the movement of the Lord in my own life in the light of my mother's thirty-year prayer vigil and the prayers of so many of God's people.

As we closed out the first two weeks of my reentry into society as a free man, Kathleen, Maceo, Joju, and I flew to Philadelphia where we were house guests of Art De Moss and his family for a week. To be accepted so openly by this white, affluent Christian family was a new and exhilarating experience for all of us. It was a style of family life that I had never really seen before. My boyhood home had been extremely turbulent, and our own family life was not exactly a model for anyone to follow. But here we saw open expression of love and patient understanding. I decided right then that this was what I wanted our home to be like.

Several weeks later, after we had returned to our home in San Francisco, I was speaking one night at the Walnut Creek Presbyterian Church and met a man who has had a marked influence on my life ever since: Ray Stedman, one of the pastors of the Peninsula Bible Church at Palo Alto, California. I was attracted to Ray first off because, for me at least, he looks more like a cowboy than a preacher—he just didn't fit the preacher mold. But aside from this, I soon discovered that Ray is a skillful and gifted Bible teacher. My avid interest in the Bible and in Bible study had been ignited months before in jail when Glenn Morrison had given me a Bible. Since then I had read and studied a great deal—especially in the Gospel of John. There was so much, though, that I didn't understand, but through Ray I've begun to learn more of the richness to be found in the Bible.

All of this has been a tremendous help to me over the past year or two as I have had the opportunity to speak on approximately fifty university campuses and eight Christian college and university campuses. In addition, I've had the opportunity to speak in scores of churches and service clubs, on television programs, in prisons, and on a one-to-one basis with former friends and followers.

In fact, I've been blessed with the chance to travel all

over the country and share my testimony with thousands of people. One brother with whom I especially enjoyed sharing was Charles Colson. At one time it would have been absolutely ludicrous to even speculate that Charles Colson and Eldridge Cleaver could ever have anything in common. There was a time when I hated him as much as I hated Richard Nixon; now Nixon is on my prayer list and Chuck Colson is my friend.

During my nine months in Alameda County Jail, well-meaning friends would send me all kinds of books, and I received several copies of Chuck Colson's *Born Again*. At first I would not even look inside the book. Even though I had become a Christian, I still had strong feelings against Colson. But one day when I was just lying around in my cell with nothing to do and absolutely bored to death, I picked up the book and started to read. Much to my amazement, I was strongly attracted to Chuck as I read my way through the book; I became convinced he was a real man and not a phony. And our mutual commitment to a ministry in prisons has cemented a supportive relationship that has been exceptionally helpful to me.

I am just now aware and becoming full of a sense of responsibility in believing that God doesn't waste his time fooling around with people unless he has something for them to do. I believe that God wants me to share the experience I have had in coming to him with others who have turned away from him. The hope of helping bring them back to him is the cause for which I now live.

In my entire life I have never been so happy and never felt so blessed. Many times people ask me if I feel as though I am being used, and I can only tell them that I am happy to be used; the worst thing in the world is to be useless. The only thing I don't like is to be misused, and I look to God to help me keep that from happening. I am thankful that even though it took me forty-one years to come out from beneath all the philosophy and science that I put upon myself, at last I found the bridge between myself and God—between myself and you. I praise the Lord for what happened and for the walk I started. I am two years old as a Christian and the future looks bright. I am here to be used until I am used up. I praise the Lord.

EPILOGUE

If I, or any members of my family, have ever been guilty of bigotry or racial prejudice—as we undoubtedly have been—our relationship these past two years with Eldridge Cleaver and his family has certainly done a great deal to obliterate this.

When Eldridge first got out of prison back in August of 1976, he, his wife, Kathleen, and their two children came and stayed with us for a time. Our whole family immediately took to them.

I soon realized that God had gifted Eldridge Cleaver with the practically unique ability of helping to unite and reconcile people—through the gospel of Christ—of various racial, religious, political, and economic

backgrounds and persuasions. In the ensuing months, I
have seen many illustrations of this, some of which
Eldridge recounts in the book you have just read.

Shortly after leaving prison and immediately following
his stay with us, Eldridge was part of a unique and
poignant meeting that took place in Washington where he
and former White House hatchet man Chuck Colson,
former liberal Democratic Senator Harold Hughes, and
former Alabama Ku Klux Klan leader Tommy Terrants all
met together. I'm sure the angels in heaven rejoiced to see
such a disparate group as this praying together and loving
each other—because Jesus Christ had melded them
together.

Then there was the time in Lynchburg, Virginia, when
Jerry Falwell, pastor of Thomas Road Baptist Church,
turned over his Sunday morning pulpit to Eldridge Cleaver,
with the service being televised nationally. Following the
service, a southern policeman came up to Eldridge
backstage and proffered his hand in greeting. After
shaking hands with Eldridge, the policeman looked at his
hand and said, "Gosh, I don't think I'll ever want to wash
that hand!" When I think of what intense and total
polarization would have existed here before these two men
came to a saving knowledge of Jesus Christ, I am reminded
again of the tremendous unifying power of the gospel.

I also recall the evening when Ralph Wilkerson, pastor
of a very large church in southern California, thoughtfully
provided a police escort for Eldridge and his family
because of a bomb threat made earlier in the day when it
was learned that Eldridge would be giving his testimony
there that evening. Having a police escort was a new
experience for the Cleaver children (and I am sure for
Eldridge also!), which prompted six-year-old Maceo to ask
for an explanation of what was going on. Eldridge explained
that the police were trying to help protect them, in case

anyone wanted to hurt them. Maceo looked quizzically at his dad and exclaimed, "I thought the cops hated us!"

"No, son," Eldridge replied, "that was the *old* Eldridge Cleaver."

As an eyewitness to these incidents, I can testify to the transforming power of the gospel in the lives of Eldridge and Kathleen Cleaver, and to the dramatic changes that have resulted. So I'm delighted to be able to write these few words for him at the request of the new Eldridge Cleaver.

Eldridge, the former militant and a man who has spent almost half of his life in prison, and who is even now awaiting trial for assault with intent to kill, is now engaged in a crusade against violence.

I believe Eldridge, deep down in his own way, has always wanted to help people. He has now learned how to *really* help people, how to truly change lives, invariably for the better, through the gospel of Christ. And he has much going for him. He is extremely bright, intelligent, and articulate. Now, with Jesus Christ in his life, I am confident the Lord has a great future for him.

In the last letter I received from Eldridge, just a few days ago, he said, "Kathleen and I continue to spend time in personal study of the Bible, and feel ourselves growing in knowledge of the Lord. Also, at the Crusades office, our staff meets regularly for prayer and Bible study. This emphasis on biblical studies has become quite important to me. Just as I once studied revolutionary materials in order to direct my life, I now have a great thirst for God's Word and for his purposes. The Lord has transported me from worldly revolutions to a radical dependence on his transforming power."

Lastly for now, I'd like to request the prayers of all of Eldridge's brothers and sisters who read this book, for him and for his new life in Christ—that he might be able to know and do God's perfect and holy and wonderful will for his life, and thus optimize the tremendous potential which he has in Christ. Ever since his release from prison, he has been inundated with every conceivable kind of request, business proposition, financial lure, and temptation.

Eldridge needs our prayers because, like the rest of us, he is not perfect—just forgiven. But he has come a very long way in his spiritual pilgrimage in a very short period of time. And I can testify that he has come not only to know but to greatly love the Lord Jesus Christ and the Word of God.

Arthur S. De Moss

April 1978